YOUR DESTINY DISCOVERED

ASTROLOGY FOR BELIEVERS

DISCOVER YOUR UNIQUE GIFTS AND TALENTS THROUGH
FAITH-BASED INTERPRETATION OF THE STAR PATTERN
IN THE HEAVENS ON THE DAY YOU WERE BORN

Rose Martin

ACHIEVEMENT
PUBLICATIONS
Fayetteville, AR

Your Destiny Discovered, Astrology for Believers
By Rose Martin

Published by Achievement Publications
PO Box 3321
Bella Vista, AR United States

Email: YourDestinyDiscovered@gmail.com
Web: www.YourDestinyDiscovered.com

Edited by Charles T. Martin
Cover by Rose Martin
Three Wise Men © Can Stock Photo / kevron2001

Punctuation corrections made April 2023

The content provided herein is for educational purposes only. Every effort has been made to ensure that the content provided is accurate and helpful for the reader at publishing time. However, this is not an exhaustive treatment of the subjects. No liability is assumed for losses or damages due to the information provided. The reader is responsible for his/her own life choices and decisions. They are theirs to make.

The reader is regarded to consent to the fact that both the publisher and the author of this book are not qualified to give legal, financial, medical, psychological, psychiatric, or any other specialist advice. If you require such advice you should seek a licensed professional or, a minister. The author's service is to provide astrological information.

Dedication

Dedicated to all Believers who are searching for their
Kingdom Identity and Purpose.

To my daughter and son, Rachael and Sean who compelled me to
look higher into the Heavens for answers in my own search. To
my parents, Sigfried and Annamarie who forever inspire me. To
my husband, Charles, who stood by me throughout this entire
contrary undertaking with his never-ending love and support. To
my sister, Margret, who at the end helped me pull this all together.
And most of all, to the Lord God Almighty, Who entrusted me with
insight into His Heavens, gave me the charge to share it with the
World, and the strength and courage to do so!

Table of Contents

Forward

The Exact Time the Star Appeared

*After **Jesus was born in Bethlehem** in Judea, during the time of King Herod, **Magi** from the east arrived in Jerusalem, asking, **"Where is the One** who has been born **King of the Jews? We saw His star in the east** and have come **to worship Him,"*** **"In Bethlehem in Judea,"** *they replied...Then Herod called the Magi secretly and **learned** from them **the exact time the star had appeared.*** *Matthew 2:1,2,5,7*

There was a specific Star Pattern in the Heavens at the time when Yeshua, Jesus, was born. The pattern contained a specific Star. The time when it appeared gave the Wisemen the markers they needed to find Him. The Wisemen knew what to look for in the Heavens. They interpreted the Star Pattern in the Heavens and found the Savior.

There is a Star Pattern in the Heavens each day, and there was a Star Pattern in the Heavens at the exact time you were born. This Star Pattern reveals the story of your life and when interpreted provides great insight and guidance to finding yourself and your Kingdom Identity.

An Astronomer looks at the sky and sees the Stars. An Astrologer looks at the Stars and seeks to Interpret Life on Earth. A King-Priest looks at the Stars and seeks their Spiritual and Mystical significance. They want to grow closer to the God in Heaven and live more fully in agreement with the Biblical concept of "As Above, So Below." (Matthew 6:10)

Your Destiny Discovered, Astrology for Believers instructs Born-again Believers on how to interpret their unique Star Pattern using the Divine Science of Astrology. These interpretations are founded on the Bible and its principles.

The place for Believers to start understanding their Book of Life in the Heavens is to study the Luminaries; the Sun, the Moon, and the Stars, that were hung in the Heavens on the 4th day of Creation.

In the beginning, God created the lights...
Genesis 1:14-19

*And God said, "Let there be lights in the vault of the sky to separate the day from the night, and let them **serve as signs** to mark sacred times, and days and years, and let them be lights in the vault of the sky to give light on the Earth."*
*And it was so. **God made two great lights—the greater light to govern the day and the lesser light to govern the night. He also made the stars.** God set them in the vault of the sky to give light on the Earth, to govern the day and the night, and to separate light from darkness. And God saw that it was good.*
And there was evening, and there was morning— the fourth day.

Through interpreting the position of these Heavenly Bodies at the exact time of their birth, Believers can discover the gifts, talents, and even the challenges with which they were born with as ordained by God, their Creator.

This Scripture says that God created the Sun to govern, or rule, the day, and the Moon to govern, or rule, the night. What does this mean? How does God govern through the Sun, the Moon, and the Stars? What does God govern with them? The answers to these questions will unfold in the following chapters.

God's Voice is going out into all the Earth…
Psalm 19:1-6

The heavens declare the glory of God; the skies proclaim the work of his hands. *Day after day* ***they pour forth speech****; night after night* ***they reveal knowledge****. They have no speech; they use no words; no sound is heard from them. Yet* ***their voice goes out into all the Earth, their words to the ends of the world.*** *In the heavens God has pitched a tent for the sun. It is like a bridegroom coming out of his chamber, like a champion rejoicing to run his course. It rises at one end of the heavens and makes its circuit to the other nothing is deprived of its warmth.*

The Heavens declare the work of God's hands and continue to speak to us every day!

In the following pages we will see that throughout the Bible, and in the lives of our Spiritual forefathers, including Adam, Abraham, Moses, Jacob, Joseph and Yeshua, the Heavens were recognized as speaking for God. We, as modern-day Born-again Believers, should not be strangers to the voice and message of God as contained in the Heavens.

"...I will no longer be silent.

"Clearly, negative misstatements about Astrology are based not on factual evidence from the Bible, but solely upon untruths and innuendo that continue to be passed along from one misinformed person to another. Please refer to the Biblical passages cited in this book in support of God's celestial plan that includes Astrology. (Stephan 122-123)"

Preface

I Was Taught Astrology Was Wrong

As a Believer I was taught that Astrology was wrong and was not for Believers, so I did not consider it something to delve into. After 30 years of salvation and serving the Lord with all of my heart, soul, and mind, I was earnestly searching for answers to some serious questions I had about my life and faith. The Lord began to answer my questions in an unexpected way. He showed me the most wonderous things in the Heavens that He created, and they included Astrology!

My husband Charles and I were highly active in our faith and service to the Lord. We were ordained ministers and held leadership positions in the churches we attended. In the late 1980's we discovered the Hebrew roots of our faith and began to have an interest in Israel and the Jewish people.

In 2005, after earnestly seeking the answer to 'Why are we not keeping the Sabbath, when the Word says we should?', the Lord led us to The Tabernacle of Praise, a Messianic Jewish and Christian congregation, where we discovered the feasts and festivals. We studied the Torah, learned Biblical Hebrew, and Davidic Worship under Rabbi Jeremy Storch. We were ordained as Messianic Pastor and Minister and fully embraced the Messianic Jewish faith and kosher lifestyle. We kept the Sabbath.

After several years I began to ask, 'Why do we celebrate all the Feasts of the Lord and not the New Moon, when the Word says we

11

should?' I prayed, wondered, and kept seeking the Lord for an answer. The question kept coming up in my mind.

The answer came during a time when my husband and I were living in our motorhome in 2016 and were traveling around the country. We were in Waco, Texas during one of our stops. There we toured a Christian homestead that had a bookstore. There was a home-schooling section which included books about the Solar System. I wondered if I could learn something about the Moon from these books. Since the Christian Homeschoolers were teaching their children about the Solar System, I thought it would be OK to begin to learn more about it. I bought some books thinking they could teach me something about the Moon, and maybe this would provide me with some additional understanding of what the New Moon festival was about.

As I continued to study the Solar System and the Moon, the Lord began to reveal to me how they all fit together. He showed me that the Moon was a marker in the Heavens that gave signs that man could interpret. Each new Month provided a new message. I learned that the Moon was linked to the Sun and to the other Planets. They were all used in Astrology. I wondered; how could Astrology be so wrong when it is God speaking to man through His Heavens?

My resistance to learning about Astrology was extremely high. For over 30 years after my radical conversion at my salvation, I was taught Astrology was not of God. Before I was saved, I was on the path of becoming a full-time Astrologer. I helped people with compatibility questions, and I was on my way to a career in this field. However, after I accepted the Lord as my Savior, I threw it all away, literally. The Church told me it was wrong. I loved the Lord so very much and did not want to do anything that would displease Him.

I trusted those in Church leadership and threw away my library of Astrology books and Charts. I put it all behind me and never looked back, even though I knew it held answers to people's personalities. Everything was new to me as a Christian, so if the Church told me God says it was wrong, I must not understand something about it and believed what they told me. Astrology became wrong in my mind. So, when the Lord started bringing it up to me, I resisted it for a long time, thinking I was not understanding Him correctly. But He persisted and I slowly went forward inch by inch. The Lord began to give me more of a desire to learn more about His Heavens.

I wondered if Astrology could help people find the answers to questions for which they were searching about their purpose and identity. But was Astrology OK for Christian Believers? I decided to ask a Believer I knew who had moved to Israel to see if she knew what people in Israel thought about Astrology. She told me that many people in Israel have their 'Mazal' read and that she had hers read several times. I thought if they do it in Israel, the land of God, it must not be wrong. So, I took another step forward.

One day while in Corpus Christi, Texas, I was standing by the kitchen sink of our RV, asking the Lord if He really wanted me to study Astrology. At that moment it was as if I was standing in the darkness of the Heavens with the Stars all around, ready to step into the unknown. Should I really be studying this Lord? Is it really of you? Will this help people? I felt His YES in my mind and spirit. I saw myself getting ready to take a step into the vastness of Heaven believing the Lord would catch me. I looked up into the Heavens and felt Him lifting me up as I took a step. I felt the blessing from the Lord to begin to study Astrology and made the decision to answer His call. I asked the Lord to always guide and direct me through His Holy Spirit and not let me go astray, as I never wanted to do anything against His Will.

This began my intensive study. I bought one book after the other and did nothing but study this amazing science. With every new step I stopped and asked, is this still of You Lord? Every step He said yes. There were definitely some forbidden areas I came across which I immediately felt in my spirit were not right and I disregarded them. When I felt uncomfortable, I stopped and prayed and waited to go forward. I let the new discoveries sink in and match up with what I had learned in my 30 years of daily study of the Word. If it matched, I went forward, if not, I stopped.

I wondered if I could find the woman who was teaching the Astrology classes I took 30 years prior. I did not remember her name, only the city where I took the classes. I searched online and found her! Her name was Sophia Mason and discovered she had written several books. I could pick up from where I left off! The

13

concepts began to come back to me, and I remembered the basics I had learned and began to build on them.

Most every book written about Astrology was written from a secular viewpoint, not giving God the glory. The principles were there, but the Lord was not acknowledged in the way that He should be. There were many New Age concepts I had to sort out and reconcile to God's ways.

I needed to make sure I was on the Biblical track in my studies. I wanted to learn Astrology from a good Jewish source. It was a part of life in Israel, and everyone knew of their Mazal, or their Star Pattern, or Natal Chart. Why was it OK in Israel, and not for the Believers in the USA?

I searched for books on Jewish Astrology. I found one written by Yaakov Kronenberg called *Jewish Astrology, A Cosmic Science*. It was amazing. I contacted him and asked if he could teach me. He taught Astrology according to Jewish Law. This was exactly what I needed! He lived in Israel, but he could teach me via Skype. So, for a year, we had our weekly Astrology classes. He taught me the principles of Ancient Astrology and I received the instruction I needed to make sure I was doing it God's way and not the New Age way. I was connected directly to Israel as I was learning this Divine Science. It was a life changing experience for me.

Now I wondered, if this is so real, why is it not allowed in the Church? In my studies I discovered it was stopped by Church and political leaders for various reasons. They simply conveyed the message that it was not valid and for people to stay away from it. Almost everyone believed them without questioning, especially the Christians.

But what about the New Moon Celebration the Bible speaks of? I discovered that the New Moon that leads to the Sun and the rest of the Solar System, all lead to where the Signs of the Times are in the Heavens. I began to see more of the reasons why leaders wanted to block the people from this vital information.

Once I got the go ahead from the Lord, I continued to get confirmation that I was on the right path. I devoured every piece of information I could get about Astrology. The older, more Ancient the source the better. I studied from morning to night seven days a week. For three years the RV we lived in became my private study sanctuary in which the Lord showed me how to interpret the Heavens.

During one of my times with the Lord, I wondered why He had me leave it all behind and now, after 30 years, why He began to reveal Astrology to me again. God showed me that after 30 years of diligently studying the Word, I now had the foundation on which to understand Biblical Astrology. If I had continued back then, it would have been from a secular viewpoint. Now, after 30 years of studying and living the Word, it would help me to discern and be able to align Astrology with God's truth.

Needless to say, no one else around me got the revelation about Astrology and the Heavens. The people from the churches I had attended all turned their backs on me. I could understand because that is where I was just a short time ago. My husband had no problem with me studying it but did not get involved himself. He kept his feet on the ground while I explored the Heavens.

It was a difficult, lonely path on which I experienced a lot of rejection. I was swimming upstream against the flow of tradition. But I knew the Lord wanted me to do it, and I knew it could help so many people. That was my driving force.

Astrology shows you who you were created to be. After learning to read my own Chart, I was reassured when I understood that the Lord made me for this! He gave me a contrary personality with the strength to go against the crowd and the desire and ability to dig deep into spiritual matters. My Mazal showed me my gifts and talents, and also the areas that would be a challenge. It showed me that this assignment would be lonely and difficult, especially at the beginning. Even though I now know this, it is still difficult. However, I am humbled knowing He has chosen me. I receive comfort and strength knowing He has not given me more than I can bear. I get excited about all of the people Astrology has already helped and all those that it will help in the future. I am honored to bring God, the Creator of the Universe, back into the interpretation and understanding of the Heavens.

The Lord has shown me that not only is Faith-based Astrology not wrong or forbidden, but that it is greatly missed. People need to know about their identities. So many people are searching for theirs. Faith-based Astrology has helped alcoholics and drug addicts discover who they are, teens who are uncertain, parents of teens, and those going through a mid-life crisis. It can help parents understand their children and people understand each other. It will help anyone wanting to know more about themselves and who they are in God's Kingdom. This knowledge will help them better fulfill their life's purpose.

My assignment from the Lord is to bring the tool of the Divine Science of Astrology back to Believers. Early in my studies the Lord showed me that He wanted me to write a book that would introduce people to Biblical Astrology. Now four years later, after over 8,000 hours of study, classes, practice, and the much-appreciated editing help and advice from my husband, the time has come. I give all glory to the Lord God, and present:

YOUR DESTINY DISCOVERED
ASTROLOGY FOR BELIEVERS

**Discover Your Unique Gifts and Talents through
Faith-based Interpretation of the Star Pattern
in the Heavens on the Day You Were Born**

I pray you will be awed and inspired by the God Who created the Heavens, and amazed when you discover who He created you to be!

Rose Martin
Fayetteville, Arkansas
May 24, 2020 3:44am
1 Sivan 5780

Introduction

Your Star Pattern in the Heavens

What Does the Exact Time You Were Born Say About You?

Imagine if, at the moment you were born, your parents took a picture of the Heavens at that exact time so, when you grew up, you would know what the Heavens looked like. The picture showed the many Stars shining brightly in the Heavens forming various patterns with single Stars and clusters, some of which were brighter and more noticeable than others.

Imagine if, at the moment you drew your first God-ordained breath, and as the doctor was recording the time of birth on your medical Chart, the Angels in Heaven were taking a picture of the Heavens at the same exact moment and noting the Stars and their Patterns in your Book of Life!

This is only an illustration of how your Book of Life might be opened and recorded, and to visualize how the Stars in the Heavens can have symbolism and meaning in your life. It is true, however, that on the day you were born, the Heavens were arranged in a particular way, and the view at the exact time and place of your birth marks your unique Star Pattern. According to Biblical reality, God knew this pattern in advance and placed you here on Earth at the exact moment you were to be born. (Jeremiah 1:5)

Your Natal Chart is like a .jpg image of the configuration of the Heavens at the exact time you were born. Amazingly, from this Star Pattern, you can get insight into who you are and who you were created to be!

God created markers in the Heavens which include the Sun, the Moon, and the Stars. In the Bible these are called the Heavenly Lights, or Luminaries. We read again from Genesis Chapter One:

*God made **two great lights—the greater light to govern the day and the lesser light to govern the night. He also made the stars**. God set them in the vault of the sky to give light on the earth, to govern the day and the night, and to separate light from darkness.*
Genesis 1:16-18

The way these markers, or Luminaries, were arranged in the Heavens on the day you were born make up your Mazal, the Hebrew word for a 'Map of the constellations.' This Map shows the physical and spiritual reality of the Heavens. Your Mazal will reveal your unique personality. It is like a Blueprint for your life.

The Mazal is also called a Natal Chart, Star Map, Horoscope, Blueprint of the Heavens. One could say it contains the Table of Contents for your Book of life. As you interpret your Mazal, it will give you great insight into the promises and potentials with which you were born. It will provide you with amazing answers to important meaning of life questions. As Rabbi Joel C. Dobins, a Rabbi and Jewish Astrologer, writes:

> "A horoscope is usually defined as a 'Map of the Heavens, for the date and time of one's birth, as viewed from the place of one's birth.' To this definition of the horoscope, our Israelite ancestors would add the following words: ...'which will reveal the will of God for the person, and the place of the person in the balance of man, God, and universe' (Dobins 29)."

Your Natal Chart is your signature in the Heavens. The moment that you took your first breath, it was noted and God's destiny for your life on Earth began. And your book continues to be written even today!

Your Map of the Heavens is a powerful tool to help you navigate your life. You can use the same tools our Biblical forefathers used to discover the talents with which you were born, what your life's path is, what motivates you, and how you interact with the world. These tools are the Sun, the Moon, and the Stars, all of which God put into place at Creation (Genesis 1:14)

Using the Sun, and the Moon, and the Stars that were created on the fourth day as markers, and acknowledging God as the Creator of all, you have the keys that will help unlock your understanding of the destiny and purpose God created for your life. Where these markers appear on your Natal Chart will give you insight into your Kingdom Identity and a starting point to understanding your purpose.

Through the Divine Science of Astrology, you have the opportunity to discover the uniqueness of who you were created to be; your personality, talents, strengths, even your weaknesses. This insight is designed to help you fulfill the plan the Lord has for your life!

As you learn about your life and destiny, you will grow more confident and secure, knowing you are walking hand in hand with the Creator of the Universe. This understanding adds a closer and more connected dimension to your walk with the Lord that was not possible before. **It is something that is available for every Believer!**

Once you discover and interpret these Luminaries, these Heavenly lights, on your Map of the Heavens you begin an amazing journey! You can seek the Lord, read Scriptures, think about your life and experiences you have had and see how they relate to what you have discovered about yourself. How do they fit? Are they some of the pieces of the puzzle you have been searching for? Do your efforts and training support these discoveries? Then as you get more understanding of your make up based on these interpretations you can begin to fine tune your walk with the Lord using the new insight you received.

The Heavens are filled with amazing insights into the person God created you to be!

Let the journey begin!

Who Is This Book For?

Your Destiny Discovered, Astrology for Believers is for everyone who wants to know more about the gifts and talents with which they were born and to better fulfill their life's purpose. It is for those who want to discover more about themselves. They do not need to, or care to, know how Astrology works. It is also for those who are interested in learning the fundamentals of how the Divine Science of Astrology functions. This introductory book accomplishes both.

Born-again Christian and Messianic Jews, the One New Man in faith, are all searching for answers about their lives and faith walk. Believers want to be part of the great work of reclaiming and spreading the Light of the Lord in the Mountains of Influence in this world. Biblical Astrology is designed to reveal to them the skills and talents they possess that support their calling in their work. These revelations bring people closer to God and His power and gives them an intimate understanding of who He created them to be.

Your Destiny Discovered, Astrology for Believers is a guidebook for Born-again Believers in Yeshua ha Mashiach, Jesus the Messiah, who seek answers to important life questions. They continue to seek God for answers, but they still have many unanswered questions.

What is my purpose? Am I doing what I am supposed to be doing? Why is everything so hard? What am I doing here anyhow?

I am having a mid-life crisis! I am confused about my life! Who am I? Which of the Seven Mountains should I be on? What is my Kingdom Identity?

This book unlocks the answers to these questions! It introduces the Born-again Believer to the Divine Science of Astrology from a safe, Biblical perspective so that they can explore the wonder of the Heavens at work in their lives.

This is also a book for those Believers who have already started to study Astrology but want to learn more about its Biblical origin and interpretation.

This book is for anyone who wants to learn how to read their Natal Charts and finally discover who they are!

The World is a confusing place. Believers today want reassurance that they are fulfilling their call. They need to know more about their personality and purpose. They want to discover their Kingdom Identity. Some have started to see postings and ads written about Astrology and want to know if it is of God. They wonder, "Is it safe to study? Does God approve of this for His children? Can the Heavens really give answers? How does it work? How can it even work?"

Some Believers want to know more about Astrology but are unsure how to start or where to learn in a way that agrees with their faith in God. Most of the books (in English) about Astrology are written from a New Age or secular viewpoint. Born-again Believers have been instructed to avoid these viewpoints, leaving them with little foundation to begin their search of the subject. Astrology has been lumped in with New Age Spirituality which is contrary to Biblical beliefs. Astrology has lost its Biblical roots.

Because of misclassifications and misunderstandings, Astrology has been kept from Believers by Church doctrine for hundreds of years. In the 1960's Astrology began a comeback, but it is still declared evil and forbidden by many in the Church. As a result, Astrology has fallen into New Age hands and their beliefs have removed the Biblical background and the Divinity of the Creator God from the study of Astrology. The Church has been left behind in bringing this Ancient study back to the forefront.

It is interesting to note that the Divine Science of Astrology was never banned or removed from the Jewish culture. Only in the Christian culture is the study of it banned.

To be clear, the Astrology used by the Biblical forefathers is not channeling, psychic readings, clairvoyance, fortune telling or the like. It is a Divine Science designed by God to communicate with mankind. Faith-based Astrology is part of the Believer's spiritual heritage.

Through *Your Destiny Discovered, Astrology for Believers,* Born-again Believers who have an interest in discovering the depths of their Mazal, can do so using a faith-based source. *Your Destiny Discovered, Astrology for Believers* is written from a Born-again Christian, Messianic Jewish, One New Man Believer point of view. It keeps God on His throne and respects His Word as it explores the study of the Signs in the Heavens through Astrology.

It is time to put aside the misunderstandings and put this valuable gift, this Divine Science, back into the hands of Believers so they can use it to develop a fuller relationship with God and grow into all He created them to be. Intuition, prophecy, and spirituality are increasing in this Third Day Revelation Age. Desire for increased insight into the Believer's walk with the Lord is growing stronger. Deeper answers are needed.

More than ever young people need to know who they were created to be. Children born since 2011 are born with more of a spiritual hunger and capacity than any other recent generation. Everyone wants to know more of God and experience His Love and Peace in ever increasing ways. Astrology is one tool that God provides to be able to know Him more intimately.

The principles of Jewish Astrology are built on the Bible. Jewish Astrology follows a tradition that has been handed down from generation to generation emphasized from the time of Abraham, through the Oral Law and Writings. This is the foundation Astrology is built on. It is based on and founded by God, the Creator. The first Natal Chart in Jewish Astrology was that of Adam, Adam Ha Rishon, the first man and it still serves as a template today.

"All Jewish Astrology, all of esoteric Jewish Astrology is based on an understanding of this Chart, the Chart of the First Man, that in Hebrew we call him Adam HaRishon, the First Man (Kronenberg 215)."

God wants Believers to know how to interpret the Heavens. By understanding the qualities of the Mazal of the first Man and Woman that God created, Believers can gain an understanding of themselves. As they learn to read the Heavens, they learn about God's cycles and His handiwork in their lives. They will learn more about their Kingdom Identity on this Earth and in Heaven. The more Believers know about His Heavens, the closer they will grow to Him. The Heavens are meant to draw people to Him, not to push them away.

Your Destiny Discovered, Astrology for Believers is an introduction to interpreting Natal Charts. While it does include Biblical background and Scripture validating the Believer's access to the Heavens, its focus is not on presenting an in-depth study of the history and Scriptural foundation of Astrology. If you want detailed, in depth, verse by verse evidence on which to build your knowledge and faith of the Biblical background of Astrology, there are several very thorough books that are recommend for your studies.

To Rule Both Day and Night, by Rabbi Joel C. Dobin, and ***Astrology for Christians***, by Suzan Stephan. Both provide the Biblical background, Scripture, and excellent information needed to understand, believe, and trust in Jewish Astrology. For an esoteric insight and viewpoint, ***Jewish Astrology, A Cosmic Science***, by Yaakov Kronenberg is an excellent deeply spiritual book. Through these exceptional foundational writings, further Scriptural proof of what is presented in this book, ***Your Destiny Discovered, Astrology for Believers***, is gained.

This guidebook, ***Your Destiny Discovered, Astrology for Believers,*** teaches Believers how to understand their Birth Chart in a way that agrees with Astrology's Biblical foundation. It uses terminology acceptable to Christian beliefs and acknowledges the God of Abraham, Isaac and Jacob, Yeshua His Son, and the Holy Spirit as Helper. It views God as Creator and ruler over all the

Heavens and the Earth. There is none like Him and none above Him. This is the God that is sought after in this study of the Divine Science of Astrology.

This God has also provided Believers with instructions on how to live their lives to the fullest and how to overcome any challenges or obstacles that are shown in their Natal Charts. Believers live above them through the Word of God found in the Holy Bible. The Word contains the instructions for living that have been given by our loving Father in Heaven to His children.

By interpreting the personal signature of their lives as shown in the Heavens, Believers will start receiving the answers they have been searching for! They will get the keys to understanding their identity and purpose in God's Kingdom that they were unable to find anywhere else. They will have a new reverence for the Lord, that will lead them to a closer walk with the Him. They will experience more fulfillment, peace, and happiness in their lives. Their Heavenly Star Pattern holds the answer. Knowing how to read the Heavens will make this Pattern real.

Your Destiny Discovered, Astrology for Believers is for Born-again Believers who are searching for answers to important questions about their lives. As the Hebrew roots of the Christian faith are being rediscovered and brought back by following God's calendar and celebrating the Biblical Feasts and Festivals, so should the understanding of the Signs in the Heavens that are also a fundamental part of the Hebrew roots and spiritual heritage.

It is time for Believers to learn how to read the Heavens and get the answers they have been searching for through Faith-based Astrology!

Faith-based Astrology

What is Faith-based Astrology?

Faith-based Astrology is the key aspect that distinguishes the teaching provided in this book, *Your Destiny Discovered, Astrology for Believers,* from secular or New Age Astrology. Faith-based Astrology uses Bible Doctrine as the basis for understanding and interpreting the physical order of the Heavens and the spiritual meaning of the Planet and Star Patterns. It uses traditional methods of interpretation as taught by our spiritual forefathers.

Through our individual relationship with God through His Son, Yeshua, Jesus, we each have access to understanding the spiritual realms, including the Heavens. (John 14;6, Romans 5:2, Hebrews 10:10). Yeshua opened the door to give us access to the Throne Room of God, which includes the Heavens. We have been granted access to new heights of spiritual understanding.

Through the Biblical interpretation of Astrology, we are able to learn the language of the Heavens that God created. We can understand Him and our lives on this Earth in a fuller and more meaningful way.

Faith-based Astrology acknowledges that God is the Creator of the Heavens. We recognize the Sun, the Moon, and the Stars work in accordance with His Will and purpose, but we do not give them power over our lives. We do not idolize the Heavens but use the markers as the tools God provided to help guide us on our journey. We give God the glory and do not make the Heavens idols to be worshipped.

Everything in Heaven is created and designed to worship God. That is also true for all the Earth.

Praise him, all his angels; praise him, all his heavenly hosts.
Praise him, Sun and Moon; praise him, all you shining stars.
Praise him, you highest Heavens and you waters
above the skies. Psalm 148:2-4

A Divine Science with Structure

Faith-based Astrology is a Divine Science based on the structured and orderly operation of the Universe as God created it in eternity past. There is a master plan for everything, and everything fits the Master's Sovereign Plan and purpose. In God's plan, He leaves Man some space for his input, called free-will.

We can see two of the ways God runs the world. One is the Fixed, structured way that operates by specific scientific rules that are constant and unchanging. This structure has been documented by scientific studies and proof ranging from the atoms of the Elements of Matter to Quantum Physics.

There are physical, static components to our Earth and in our Solar System. There are predictable cycles that have been built into our World and all of God's Universe. These include the cycles of the Sun, the Moon, and the Solar System that surround our Earth. They determine the Day, Night, Months, Seasons, and Years. Since everything was created by God, every part of it displays an attribute of God in some way.

In addition to the orderly Fixed operating system that forms the backdrop of our lives, there is also the serendipitous, spiritual, mystical, prayer activated, individual, free-will component of the plan. This component is the space God gives man to exercise the free-will needed to live and learn how to operate within the rules of the Fixed structure into which he was born. It combines the Fixed structure of the Heavens with the somewhat unpredictable life on Earth.

Our interaction with God helps us navigate the two as we live our lives on Earth. They work together. The Sovereign Will of God and the free will of man combine to accomplish God's predetermined plan for mankind.

God has made the Heavens and its patterns a living work. They are alive with continual precise movements, like a master clock with each Planet in our Solar System having its position and purpose as created by God. The movements in the Heavens relate to our lives on this Earth. Each Planet that God placed in our Solar System is active in the physical and spiritual realms of Heaven and Earth.

He determines the number of the Stars and calls them each by name. Psalm 147:4

The symbolic meanings of the Heavens were given by the God of Abraham, Isaac, and Jacob, to our Spiritual Ancestors. The most famous was Father Abraham, who was called out of idolatry to purify His understanding of the Heavens and bring them under ECHAD, one God, not the many inferior gods of his natural father.

> "...how did he (Abraham) become the first person to believe in one G-d? He was meditating on the Planets and he said to himself that there must be a higher force behind the Planets. It's not possible that they are directing the world by themselves. In other words, through Astrology, he came to the realization of G-d. How can the Planets run history? How can the Planets determine what is going to happen? He saw behind everything and came to a really deep conclusion that maybe once existed or got lost but whatever...He came to the realization of G-d. The founder of Judaism was an Astrologer who came to the realization of G-d through Astrology. Wonder of wonders. But that is what is written in the Talmud (Kronenberg 218)".

According to Jewish Tradition, God saw that Abraham recognized Him as the Sovereign true God, and thus entrusted him with an abundance of information about the Heavens He created. This wisdom is written in Father Abraham's Ancient Hebrew writing

29

entitled *Sefer Yetzirah - The Book of Creation*. Father Abraham was the first Astrologer. He read the symbolisms in the Heavens with skill. The book *Sefer Yetzirah* also speaks about the Divine Science of Astrology along with other spiritual insights as God taught it to Abraham.

In the age-old tradition, the pattern of the Sun, the Moon, and the Fixed (Constellations) and Wandering (Planets) Stars at the time of the baby's first breath, were noted from the Map of the Heavens and documented. This pattern is called their Mazal in Hebrew.

This moment marked the beginning of his life on Earth. Symbolically, the Book of Life for this individual's time on Earth was opened and the Star Pattern in the Heavens served as a Blueprint for the personality and the life events to come.

In the way that only the God of all Creation would know precisely how this is done, we can envision when at the moment we took our first breath of life, our physical bodies were linked to our spiritual Book of Life in Heaven. This is our Book which was written and planned for us by the Creator before time began.

I Praise you I am fearfully and wonderfully made. My frame
was not hidden from you when I was made in the secret place,
when I was woven together in the depths of the Earth. Your eyes
saw my unformed body; all the days ordained for me were
written in your book before one of them came to be.
Psalm 139:14-16

Each Book of Life also contains blank pages where new events will be added during our lifetime. As we live our lives, all the activities, routines, studies, prayers, victories, disappointments, and tears will be recorded. (Psalm 139:15-16, Revelation 20:12)

Individuals may reference their Map of the Heavens, or Mazal, as often as necessary to help understand new aspects of their personalities and the life tools they have been given. It is an evolving process. Not everything is revealed at once. It is on a need-to-know basis. God keeps things hidden until it is time to reveal them. As we walk together with God our Creator, living the life we have been sent here to live, more and more of His plan is revealed.

We were each born at the exact moment we were destined to be according to God's plan for our lives. Our birth and its time and place were not by chance. As Albert Einstein said, "God does not play dice with the universe." The Divine Science of Astrology seeks to document that exact moment, and then use what we have learned to give God the glory and to fulfill the purpose for which He sent us to this Earth.

> *Before I formed you in the womb I knew you...*
> *Jeremiah 1:5a*

Believers are Above the Planets but Not Above God

As important as the Stars in the Heavens are in the plan of God, we as Believers are not bound by the Stars. We operate above them through faith in and obedience to the Word of God. We are above, seated at the right hand of God with Yeshua. (Colossians 3:1-2)

As we have already learned, Abraham, the first Hebrew, the founder of the Jewish faith and forefather of the Messiah, was a respected astrologer. The Jewish Sages say that Abraham saw in the Stars that he and his wife Sarah were not only destined to be childless, but that they had physical infertility issues.

According to Jewish tradition, God told Abraham to look to the Heavens. Abraham watched as God moved the Planetary Pattern which then gave them the ability to conceive. God changed their destiny to show that He is above the Heavens and the Stars. God made Abraham and Sarah into new creations above the Stars and not subject to the Planetary influences.

God warned them not to make the Planets their idols or rulers. Instead they were to cling to a simple faith in God. Abraham did that, and became the father of Ishmael and Isaac, the patriarch of many great nations and a part of the lineage of Yeshua.

Rebbe Nachman of Breslev, the well-known founder of the Breslov Hasidic dynasty, teaches that "when a person clings to pure and simple faith and thereby connects to God, he or she rises above nature and above the influence of the Stars, since God is above nature."

The Stars do not control us. As Believers, we are new creations, grafted into Israel, and Israel is above the Stars. (2 Corinthians 5:17) As grafted in Believers, we are joined with Israel on this.

Jewish tradition states that Israel is beyond the Planetary influences and that God nullifies the power of the Stars for them. Their lives are not bound by the Stars. The reason Israel is not bound by the Stars is because of God's Word. When they keep God's Word, they are above the Heavens.

Israel is above the Stars and through belief in and obedience to Yeshua this also applies to Believers. Believers are above the Stars spiritually when we live according to the Word and the teaching of Yeshua, the Messiah. The Apostle Paul teaches us:

I ask that the eyes of your heart may be enlightened, so that you may know the hope of His calling, the riches of His glorious inheritance in the saints, and the surpassing greatness of His power to us who believe. These are in accordance with the working of His mighty strength, which He exerted in Christ when He raised Him from the dead and seated Him at His right hand in the Heavenly realms, far above all rule and authority, power and dominion, and every name that is named, not only in this age, but also in the one to come. And God put everything under His feet and made Him head over everything for the Church, which is His body, the fullness of Him who fills all in all. Ephesians 1:18-23

And God raised us up with Christ and seated us with Him in the Heavenly realms in Christ Jesus, in order that in the coming ages He might display the surpassing riches of His grace, demonstrated by His kindness to us in Christ Jesus. For it is by grace you have been saved through faith, and this not from yourselves; it is the gift of God, not by works, so that no one can boast. For we are God's workmanship, created in Christ Jesus to do good works, which God prepared in advance as our way of life. Ephesians 2:6-10

We are seated at the right hand of God with Yeshua in the Heavenly realms and therefore we can approach Almighty God with confidence. (1 John 5:14-15)

We, as Believers, can pray to God and seek His help, comfort, and will for every circumstance of our lives. When we encounter difficulties in our lives, we can seek God directly. We walk with Him and trust in Him to bring us through. We can also ask God to provide insight into the meaning of the Heavens through Astrology. We can use this information as a road map for our lives.

We can also pray to ask God to reveal the successes that can be ours and to seek His help to overcome the apparent obstacles that may be in the way. We are above the Planets because of our relationship with God through Yeshua and the power of His Word. His Word was given to us to help us navigate our road map and to live our lives victoriously while overcoming any weaknesses or any problems that may present themselves.

Faith-based Astrology is not fortune-telling. We have free-will and that is not removed by the information revealed in the Heavens. Instead, Faith-based Astrology interprets the symbols and patterns of the Planetary arrangements to learn the cycles of God which give us insight into our gifts, talents, and even obstacles so that we can better live our lives and fulfill God's purpose for us.

Our Natal Charts show us a Map of the Heavens to give us guidance about our personality, character, and motivation. However, we are not on auto pilot in driverless cars! We still must do the driving!

The Heavens are where we rule and reign with the Lord. But we must remember that God is above all. We are not higher. No one is higher than God. Remember that Satan wanted to sit higher than God Himself. But Satan was cast down.

"You said in your heart, 'I will ascend to heaven; above the Stars of God I will set my throne on high; I will sit on the mount of assembly in the far reaches of the north; I will ascend above the heights of the clouds; I will make myself like the Most High.' But you are brought down to Sheol, to the far reaches of the pit."
Isaiah 14:13-15 ESV

Idolatry Is Forbidden

While observing the Signs in the Heavens is permitted, Scripturally, we ARE warned about idolatry. We are warned against worshipping the Heavens and making them gods:

And when you look up to the sky and see the Sun, the Moon and the Stars--all the Heavenly array--do not be enticed into bowing down to them and worshiping things the LORD your God has apportioned to all the nations under heaven.
Deuteronomy 4:19

Acknowledge and take to heart this day that the LORD is God in Heaven above and on the Earth below. There is no other.
Deuteronomy 4:39

Faith-based Astrology attributes all strength and power to God, the God of Abraham, Isaac, and Jacob. The Planets and the Solar System have no power other than what God has given them to fulfill the purpose for which they were created. Faith-based Astrology has its roots in the Old Testament Hebrew Scriptures and the teaching of the Patriarchs. Abraham was not the only one that knew how to interpret the Heavens.

In addition to Abraham, there were Job, Joseph, and Daniel to name a few. Joseph had a profound influence over Egyptian Astrology. Daniel was an influential astrologer in Ancient Babylon. Many have communicated with God using Biblical Astrology.

The teaching and understanding of the Heavens were passed down from generation to generation for thousands of years. However, for many centuries of recent history, the teaching of this Divine Science was interrupted because of religious factors some dating back to Constantine.

In recent days Astrology has been making a comeback, but because it was banned by religious regulations it has come back surrounded by the influence of Egyptian and Roman mythology. Modern popular Astrology came back in the early 1900's but was classified as fortune telling and was again banned by the Church.

Its rich Biblical heritage was lost. The guidance the Heavens provided was unavailable. The hidden manna was there, but no one was allowed to see it.

Now this Ancient truth is coming to the forefront again. Now we have access to more of the Ancient Hebrew books and texts that have been discovered. Some of them have been translated into English and are available for us to study and learn. Traditional Astrology is making a great comeback, even with modern Astrologers. They see the pure truth and insight into personality and purpose is now even clearer. However, most modern Astrologers still do not acknowledge the God of the Bible. They practice a form of godliness but deny its power. (2 Timothy 3:5)

Being able to go back to Ancient Hebrew Biblical records and find the true meaning and purpose of Astrology and combining it with solid Spirit-led Biblical doctrine and Third Day Revelation, the power of the knowledge of the message in the Stars can bring Believers a new level of intimacy with and understanding of the Lord.

Through re-examination of the Scriptures we can see that Astrology in itself was not condemned. It was the idolatry that resulted in many people's lives from its study. Astrology is a tool – an accurate tool. Therefore, this tool is thought to have power. The power needs to be attributed to the correct source.

The power Astrology holds is the power of God. It is this power that is at work in our lives through His divine plan and Providence. It is this power of God we seek to understand and to use it for His glory.

The Israelites knew how to read the Heavens and their Mazal. God communicated with them through it. But when the Israelites began to worship the Sun, the Moon, the Stars - the Heavens themselves, and not the Creator of the Heavens Himself, they were told to stop. They were idolizing the created and not the Creator.

In the same way today, God does not want us to look at the Heavens if we do not handle them in the proper way. If we believe that the Planets are controlling our lives, rather than keeping times, showing cycles, and giving us insight into those times and cycles, then we will have also missed the point. We will think they are gods or may be led to think that we have no responsibility for our actions. Believers may think that Satan is behind the Heavens and the Planets. This is a misunderstanding of the Heavens.

Removing God from the picture is what cannot be tolerated! What is welcomed by God is to revel in amazement at Him and His Creation in the Heavens! To give Him all the glory!

He is the Maker of the Bear and Orion, the Pleiades and the constellations of the south. Job 9:9

Can you bind the chains of the Pleiades? Can you loosen Orion's belt? Can you bring forth the constellations in their seasons or lead out the Bear with its cubs?
Do you know the laws of the Heavens?
Can you set up God's dominion over the Earth?
Job 38:31-33

The Landscape of the Heavens

Setting the Stage

Looking outward from the Earth, on a clear night we see the Stars around us. We see clusters of Stars and recognize some of their formations such as the Big Dipper, the Little Dipper, North Star, Andromeda, Orion, and such. Each Star is named by God (Psalm 147:4). These Stars are part of the universe that we live in and their patterns are unique to this Earth.

With some thought we recognize that the Heavens did not appear out of nowhere by accident but are the result of a carefully orchestrated design. We begin to realize that God created these patterns in the Heavens for a purpose that was more than just to display His beauty and create inspiration and awe. We can begin to see the pictures and patterns and see that there are cycles and time relationships in the Heavens.

The patterns themselves tell us many wonderful stories of God and Redemption. The constellations display the Plan of God in human history from the Garden of Eden to the future Millennium. The Gospel of Yeshua ha Mashiach, Jesus the Messiah, is portrayed from Virgo, the Virgin birth, to Leo, the Lion of the Tribe of Judah, Who will return at the Second Coming and rule for a thousand years. Books such as *The Witness of the Stars*, by E. W. Bullinger, give excellent explanations in fascinating detail of the Story of the Gospel displayed in the patterns of the constellations.

In addition to the Gospel, the Heavens speak of events on the Earth as seen through the Signs in the Heavens. The Planets and

Stars above the Earth do not send vibrations to us, but they do show us a Heavenly perspective of what is happening here on the Earth. They speak in a spiritual, esoteric language that can be learned over time. We begin by building a foundation of knowledge of the Word of God as the base for all learning and understanding of the principles of the Heavens.

The Heavens have both a physical component and a spiritual, metaphorical, metaphysical component. In order to get our bearings, let us look at the layout of the physical and scientific component.

The Horizon, the Equator, and the Ecliptic

In the Heavens there are three circles that are used by Astrologers to fix the position of the Planets relative to the Earth. They are the Horizon, the Equator, and the Ecliptic.

Briefly, the Horizon is the line at which the Earth's surface and the sky appear to meet at any given moment. We will learn more about this in the chapter on the Rising Sign.

The Equator is an imaginary line forming a great circle around the middle of the Earth. It divides the Earth into the Northern and Southern hemispheres and is the basis from which latitude is measured.

The Ecliptic is an imaginary circle, which is marked out by the Sun as it seems to travel around the Earth above the equator. It contains the constellations of the Zodiac.

From the Astrological viewpoint, the Zodiac is the landscape that Sun travels through as it goes around the Earth. This path is the Ecliptic. The Ecliptic is where we will look closer now.

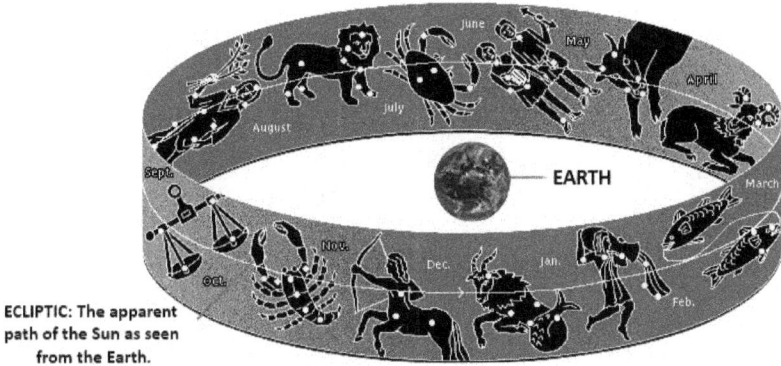

ECLIPTIC: The apparent path of the Sun as seen from the Earth.

From Earth's Viewpoint

According to science, our Sun lies at the center of our Solar System, and the Earth moves around it against the background of the Zodiac. However, from our viewpoint on the Earth as we look out into space, it is the Sun that seems to move around the Earth and from one constellation in the Zodiac to the next.

The Ecliptic the Sun appears to be traveling through is divided into 12 equal divisions of 30 degrees, each division being a named constellation. Each constellation indicates a Zodiac Sign and the 12 of them make up the 360-degree circle which surrounds the Earth.

According to Ancient Biblical writings, each of these twelve divisions represent various attributes, as designed by God during His creation. Each Zodiac Sign contains a unique richness of meaning given to it by God above, The One Who created them all. Each division is distinguishable from the other.

In addition to physical associations, such as seasons and weather, each division consists of many spiritual and esoteric attributes including Biblical features. These include the Hebrew letter spoken by God to create and form each Month, a permutation of God's Holy Name, as well as the blessings given to each of the Tribes of Israel. Each of these twelve divisions also represents a Month on the Lunar calendar.

The Number Twelve

To get an indication of the depth of meaning only one of the components of Astrology can have, let us look at these 12 equal divisions and the structures, associations, symbolisms, and additional meanings associated with the number 12 that are included in the components of each Month.

According to the Jewish Sages and the Oral Law, which was been passed down from generation to generation, Jacob's sons, who became the 12 tribes of Israel, represent 12 different soul roots from which the Jewish people descend. Each of these roots correspond with one of the 12 Signs of the Zodiac.

The number 12 also relates to the 12 Jewish months, 12 of the letters in the Hebrew alphabet that formed the months, 12 stones on the High Priest's Breastplate, 12 Apostles of Messiah, 12 baskets of leftover bread, 12 fruits of the Spirit and 12 gates of the Holy City of Jerusalem.

The number 12 also symbolizes the 12 physical attributes of man: speech, thought, progress, vision-sight, listening-hearing, health-action, sexuality-touch, smell, dream-sleep, anger, taste-eating, and laughter. There are also 12 limbs/organs of the body.

The 12 Biblical Calendar Months are: Nisan, Iyar, Sivan, Tammuz, Av, Elul, Tishrei, Cheshvan, Kislev, Tevet, Shevat, and Adar.

The 12 Zodiac signs associated with the Months, which are always in this order are: Aries, Taurus, Gemini, Cancer, Leo, Virgo, Libra, Scorpio, Sagittarius, Capricorn, Aquarius, and Pisces.

The 12 Areas of Life, or Houses, are represented in the Zodiac: self, values, communication, foundation, creativity, service, partnership, transformation, religion, career, friendships, and seclusion.

The 12 Tribes of Israel in their camping and marching order around the Tabernacle as listed in the Book of Numbers Chapter Two are: Judah, Issachar, Zebulun, Reuben, Simeon, Gad, Ephraim, Manasseh, Benjamin, Dan, Asher, and Naphtali.

Twelve is also an integral part of time. Time is organized around the number twelve. The constellations divide the night and day into 12 parts each. Our night consists of 12 hours, and our day consists of 12 hours. The solar year is composed of 12 lunar months, which are associated with the 12 constellations, or divisions.

All the Stars and all the people and all the hours in creation are represented in this number twelve! Twelve represents perfection and completion, as well as God's authority.

Twelve stands for a solid foundation for God's government. Since we as Believers are grafted into this rich Jewish family line, we are grafted into the meanings of the signs and tribes in the same way!

"If some of the branches have been broken off, and you, though a wild olive shoot have been grafted in among the others and now share in the nourishing sap from the olive root, do not consider yourself to be superior to those other branches. If you do, consider this: You do not support the root, but the root supports you. Romans 11:17-18

The number 12 is one of the most powerful numbers for humanity. If we put together all the components that make up 12, we discover rich messages from the One Who created them. Each of the 12 Zodiac Signs contains these inherent meanings and blessings and they are to be noted and celebrated at each New Moon.

Each Month provides relevant insight and guidance for Believers today. These meanings and symbols are encouraged to be studied and acknowledged each Month at the New Moon Celebrations.

For more about all that the New Moon has for Believers, please visit www.NewMoonCelebrations.com.

The rich physical and spiritual meanings of everything contained in the number 12 have an important meaning in our Natal Charts as well. The characteristics of the Month in which we are born are significant to our lives as it contains all that this number 12 represents. These qualities are a core component of our personality.

Fixed and Wandering Stars

Ancient Astrology classified the Stars as either Fixed or Wandering. The twelve Constellations that run above the Earth's ecliptic around the Earth in a 360-degree circle contain the Fixed Stars. The Fixed Stars stay Fixed in the same position in the Heavens and they make up the patterns of the Stars in the Constellations that contain the Signs of the Zodiac in the universe.

In the Heavens there are also Wandering Stars (Revelation 3:1). They are the Planets that are part of our Solar System and they wander, or travel around the Sun. In Astrological terms, from Earth's viewpoint, they travel around our Planet at various speeds in their own cycle. In addition to the Planets, astrologically the Moon and our own Sun are included in this group of Wandering Stars as they are also seen, from our viewpoint, as traveling around the Earth.

The Wandering Stars that are visible with the naked eye, and have been known since Adam, are the five Planets we know as Mercury, Venus, Mars, Jupiter, and Saturn. Physically they travel on their courses, or orbits, around the Sun as does the Earth.

Three additional Planets, whose essences were known of in Biblical times, but were not yet visibly discovered or named, are Uranus, Neptune, and Pluto. When you add the Sun and Moon to these eight Planets, we have a total of 10 'Planets' used in Astrology. These are a part of God's govern, or rule, that are spoken of in Chapter 1:14-19 of Genesis. These are also the traditional markers in our Natal Chart that tell the story of our lives. Although there are millions of Planets in the Heavens, Traditional Astrology primarily uses only the ten in association with our Solar System. While we cannot know everything, these ten give us the valuable information we need to interpret God's message for us as found in the Stars.

The movement of these Planets is constantly directed by God, Who created them, and they have a specific purpose in His plan for this world. In the spiritual realm, these Planets have significance and involve symbolic interactions with the Heavenly hosts and beings that are referenced throughout the Bible, such as angels, principalities, dominion, thrones, and powers. We will not be including their study in this book, but they are all part of the rule or government that the Word speaks of in Genesis 1:14-19.

In this book we are studying the metaphorical meaning of the ten Planets to give us understanding of their characteristics and patterns to help us to identify the gifts and talents, personality, and purpose we are to use in our service of the Lord.

The Luminaries,
The Sun, The Moon and The Stars

*There are also heavenly bodies and there are earthly bodies; but
the splendor of the heavenly bodies is one kind, and the splendor
of the earthly bodies is another. The sun has one kind of
splendor, the moon another and the stars another;
and star differs from star in splendor.*
1 Corinthians 15:40-41

The Sun, the Moon, and the Stars are the prime indicators that
God created and spoke of in Genesis. They are called the
Luminaries and are a part of the Heavenly lights. They have much
to reveal. They are three specific points in your Natal Chart which
display three key areas of your life and personality. They each
have their roles and work together to help you understand the
reality of God in your life and to fulfill the plans He has for you.
These unlock your understanding of the foundation of your
Kingdom Identity.

The symbolisms of the Sun, the Moon and the Rising Sign, or the
Luminaries, interact and blend with one another and define the
characteristics of who you are as an individual, outline your life,
activate, and color your world. They are the main energies that
drive your physical body and your overall approach to life.
Knowing about them will help you to know and understand a
tremendous amount about yourself and others! Even so, this is
only a general introduction to the richness and vastness of insight
God provides for you in the Blueprint of your life.

God has given each of these Luminaries meanings and
symbolisms that you can understand and apply to your Natal
Chart. This understanding will give you answers about who God
created you to be and will help as you discover the traits and
qualities with which you were born.

45

The Sun, physically, is the life force of the entire Earth. It is the light of the physical world. Astrologically, the Sun represents your life force. It represents your core character and goals. It reveals the particular type of skills, abilities, and experiences with which you were born. They enable you to live your life to the fullest, as designed by God.

The Moon, physically, reflects the light of the Sun and measures time along with the Sun. Astrologically, the Moon represents your emotions and your inner nature. The attributes of the Moon work together with the attributes of the Sun to help accomplish your purpose.

The Stars, physically, indicate the Sign of the Zodiac that is rising over the Eastern Horizon at any given time. Astrologically, the Stars are called your Rising Sign, or Ascendant, and is the Sign of the Zodiac which is on the Eastern Horizon at the specific moment of your birth. It reveals how you are orientated toward the world.

Your Rising Sign represents your body, appearance, and your outward personality. It indicates your outlook on life and the way you are seen by others. Your Rising Sign shows the way you present yourself to others and how you view the world. It works along with the Sun and the Moon to accomplish your purpose.

Although there are other Planets, Stars, Asteroids and other Heavenly bodies in our Solar System that are used in Astrology, in order to introduce Faith-based Astrology to you who may have never studied it before and to help you understand the key components of your Mazal as quickly as possible, this book will focus only on the prime indicators - the Sun, the Moon, and the Rising Sign - your Primary Star Pattern.

We will be starting with the Sun and its placement on your Map of the Heavens so you can gain greater insight into yourself and your life's purpose.

Your Sun Sign is an integral part of describing who you are and is the first step in learning about yourself and about others. It is also the Sign you are probably most familiar with. There are no calculations required to find out what your Sun Sign is. All you need to know is your birthdate!

The Sun,
The Giver of Life

*And God made the two great lights—**the greater light to rule the day...*** *Genesis 1:16 ESV*

Each morning the Sun rises over the eastern horizon. It represents the promise of a new day as it rises in victory from the darkness of the long night. A view of the Sunrise reminds us to reflect on the wonder and potentials of a new day. We give thanks as we begin our morning rituals and routines. We offer praise to God, seek guidance, and pray to be used in His service to others this day.

From the rising of the Sun to the place where it sets, the Name of the LORD is to be praised. Psalm 113:3

The Sun, called 'the giver of life,' is at the center of our Solar System. The Sun is the transmitter of the life to our physical body. Nothing on Earth can live without Sun. Spiritually, the Sun represents God the Creator, our Giver of Life. As God is the center of our lives, the Sun is the center of our Solar System. The Sun is the source of all light and life sustained within our Solar System.

The Sun is symbolic of God's Spirit, which is the transmitter of life to our Body, Soul, and Spirit and sustains our lives.

The LORD is God and he has made his light shine on us. Psalm 118:27a

For the LORD God is a Sun and a shield; the LORD gives grace and glory; He withholds no good thing from those who walk with integrity. Psalm 84:11 BSB

The Sun as the Symbolic Center of Your Life

In the Divine Science of Astrology, the Sun symbolizes the center of your life, as well as your spirit. It represents the vital force of your life and is the source of your will. It reveals your individuality, who and what you are at your heart level. It indicates known, as well as unknown, hidden strengths you need to develop, or weaknesses you need to overcome. It is the core of your Kingdom Identity.

Your Sun Sign provides valuable information about the foundational characteristics of your unique personality. It represents qualities which you can use and develop in a constructive way to feel good about yourself and become who you were uniquely created to be. It is the first step in discovering your destiny!

What the Sun Represents in Your Natal Chart

- Your Sun is associated with your will and identity
- It is the core of your individuality in the world
- It points toward your life's purpose, path, and destiny
- It is the source of vitality and personal power
- It is the highest expression of your true self
- It is what makes you proud- It is your ego
- The Sun points to how and where you are to 'shine' in your life

Your Sun Sign indicates the specific qualities of your Sun's energy.

The Sun's Sign

In Astrology, the position of the Sun in the Heavens is identified by its position in one of the twelve constellations. Each constellation is a Zodiac Sign. Each of the twelve Zodiac signs has its own unique qualities that filter the way the energy of the Sun shines through it.

The Zodiac Sign that the Sun occupied at the time of your birthday is called your Sun Sign. In the Natal Chart the Sun Sign reveals the unique qualities at the core of your will.

The Sun Sign identifies the primary goals and desires of your life which require your active and conscious action to accomplish. People think that they automatically live up to all that their Sun Sign qualities indicate. While many traits do come naturally, not all of them are refined to their highest level. There are imbalances.

The Sun Sign represents both the qualities of your life that you need to consciously strive to attain, and those that come instinctively. Later in this book you will see that the Moon represents traits that come more instinctively.

We are not locked into the personality of our Sun Sign. Each of us is born with the strengths and weaknesses indicated by the position of our Sun. As we live and grow, they change. They develop and adapt with us as we naturally live our lives. We can also use our free will to focus on improving our strengths and overcoming our weaknesses. This brings them into balance.

As we strive for a life where the physical, mental, and emotional are brought into harmony, we can follow the cycles of the Biblical Calendar (Jewish) year. We are helped through these spiritual guidelines God has given to us. God provides opportunities for us to grow throughout our lives. The lessons of life and the good works that God has prepared in advance for us will also refine us. (Ephesians 2:10)

Perfecting the traits of the Sun can be difficult at times, but also most rewarding. We always want to do better, especially in the area of our lives where our Sun shines. No matter how great the accomplishment, the Sun always wants to shine more brightly.

Your Pride of Life

The Sun represents your individuality. It is also called your ego. It describes the core makeup of your purpose. It represents your free will and your potential. It rules your creative urge and the pride in what you have created. Because the Sun shines so brightly in your life, it also reveals your pride of life, the area of life you take pride in. It is the area you must learn to submit to God and refine throughout your life.

Pride can be a positive or negative influence in your life. Ideally, it needs to be experienced in a way where you are 'all you can be' while balancing it with humility and submission. God's guidance through His Word and the Holy Spirit will help you to accomplish this.

Do not love the world or anything in the world. If anyone loves the world, the love of the Father is not in him. For all that is in the world—the desires of the flesh, the desires of the eyes, and the pride of life—is not from the Father but from the world. The world is passing away along with its desires, but whoever does the will of God remains forever.
1 John 2:15-17

The Sign your Sun is in shows the qualities you have to develop a healthy ego and sense of individuality. By developing the positive and constructive qualities of your Sun Sign, you will feel more complete and are more fulfilled.

The Sun in Your Natal Chart

We are all created by God and live under the same Heavens. God has made each of us with a unique blend of all the characteristics He created. We each have varying amounts of the qualities of every Zodiac Sign in our makeup. We are all beautiful in our own way. Be that as it may, we may have too much of a bad trait or too little of a good trait. This can cause challenges and imbalances in our life.

In your Chart you will have some beneficial and some difficult concentrations or combinations of these traits. When you find out what those are, you can learn to develop the positive or bring the negative into submission thereby living a more balanced life.

When you learn that most people born during the same Sun Sign will develop many of the same traits to some degree, you will be able to understand the key components of other people's personalities in a new and wonderful way. This will lead to greater harmony and understanding with your family, friends, and acquaintances. What you learn from the symbolism of the Luminaries will help you better understand yourself and others.

Keep in mind the characteristics assigned to your Sun Sign may not all be actively displayed in your life at once. You might even like another Sign's qualities better than your own! You must remember the Sun is only one component of your being. Chances are you have that quality at work in another prominent area of your Chart and that is why it resonates with you. When qualities ring true, or speak to you, they are either part of your makeup already, or ones that you are striving to improve and refine. Knowing that they are part of your makeup, even if you do not see them yet, can give you hope and a vision for the future, believing that they are still attainable.

The Sun is only one of the three Luminaries. The Moon and Rising Sign, as described later in this book, will also reveal components of your personal characteristics. These characteristics interrelate and interact. Some are stronger than others. Some will develop later in life. Therefore, it is important for you to study the characteristics of all three Luminaries and their descriptions before drawing any final conclusions about the accuracy of the characteristics described.

The descriptions will overlap. If you have your Sun in Capricorn and read the description of the Moon in Capricorn, you will often find those traits resonate with you even though your Moon may actually be in a different Sign. You can apply those additional insights to your Sun even though they are listed under the Moon Signs.

The traits of each Zodiac Sign, in this case Capricorn, are universal and will apply to the Sun, Moon and Rising Sign when in that same

Sign. The purpose and the use of the traits will be the difference. The traits will be used either by the Sun, the Moon, or the Rising Sign in their own way as they blend to make up the whole person. They can be likened to your Mind, Will and Emotion. All work together in your life. It is not easy to see where one ends and the other begins as they all work together.

There are no good Signs or bad Signs. Your Heavenly Blueprint contains each one of them, in different combinations and proportions, and they each present the opportunities and challenges you must work with throughout your life.

Let us first explore the traits and characteristics of your Sun Sign. It is the Sign with which people are most familiar. Through the description of the Sun in your Natal Chart you will gain greater insight into yourself and your life's purpose. Your Sun Sign helps bring into focus your identity, goals, and Kingdom purpose. It shows you the foundational tools and skills you have been given to use and develop in this lifetime. Insight into your Moon and Rising Signs will add to this foundational understanding and will be covered in later chapters of this book.

Defining Traits of Each Zodiac Sign

These are the guidelines for the Zodiac Sun Sign traits listed on the following pages. They define the general characteristics that the individual born under that Sun Sign will display. Each Sign is born with its strengths, weaknesses, likes and dislikes. These traits can also be considered the tools, or gifts and talents, you have available to use and develop throughout the various phases and stages of your life.

Zodiac Sign: The name of the constellation the Sun was in on the date of your birth.

Birthdate Range: The general span of birth dates is indicated for that Zodiac Sign. Look for the date range in which your birth date falls. This is your Sun Sign. If you were born at the very beginning or very end of a Sign's date range, use an ephemeris or online Zodiac Sign calendar to find the exact Sign your birth date was in that year. The Sun will definitely be in one of the Signs, but you may display some traits of each Sign since they are so close.

Sign Nature: These are the defining traits and characteristics of the Zodiac Sign, indicating the nature of your gifts and talents (Luke 19:11-27) as well as weaknesses associated with the Zodiac Sign. They are the tools given to you to use to develop during your walk on this Earth. Each of the Zodiac Signs has traits that define it and make up the foundational tools of that Sign. Symbolically, your Sun, or ego, uses the gifts and talents of the Sign it is in and uses and develops them for your life purpose. It is the fundamental way the light shines in your heart and is at the core of your being.

Fulfillment: These are areas of life that can bring fulfilment as well as challenges to your life. This also gives insight into the Mountain of Influence where your light will shine the brightest. Life is filled with joys and challenges. Overcoming challenges brings growth and fulfillment. The placement of the Sun in your Zodiac Sign highlights the challenges you are likely to face and where the victories will bring the most fulfillment.

Pride of Life: This is the area of your life in which you have the likelihood of becoming the most boastful. This is where you want to shine. You are proud of yourself in this part of your life and try to do your best. You are the center of your life in this area.

Keeping Pride in Check: These are actions and attitudes that stretch you, move you out of your comfort zone, and cause you to 'die to yourself.' Here you put yourself aside and do good for others which helps you to balance and grow. Doing this 'hurts so good' as the saying goes.

For if you live according to the flesh, you will die; but if by the Spirit you put to death the misdeeds of the body, you will live.
Romans 8:13

Challenging/Unbalanced Traits: You can be born with too much or too little of a quality. If you let your inclinations grow and get out of control in either direction it may result in difficulty or imbalance in certain areas of your life. You can learn to balance them through time with the Lord, meditating on God's Word, applying it to your life, and doing the good works (Ephesians 2:10) that have been prepared in advance for your life by The Creator. In other words, live each day as best as you can, with the best intentions, and make the most of every opportunity it provides.

...let us throw off everything that hinders and the sin that so easily entangles. And let us run with perseverance the race marked out for us...
Hebrews 12:1

Therefore, as we have opportunity,
let us do good to all people.
Galatians 6:10

Sun in Aries, March 21 – April 20

ARIES

ARIES NATURE: Adventurous, courageous, determined, confident and quick-witted. You are enthusiastic, optimistic, dynamic, and pioneering.

With your Sun in Aries you are bold and self-assertive. You were born with the will to succeed and to experience life on your own terms. You like new beginnings, are enthusiastic, and can be impulsive. You are direct in your approach and like to go forward without any opposition.

Often impatient, headstrong, and competitive, you like to be first and want to achieve your goals. You are a trailblazer. You need freedom to be able to start a new project whenever the inspiration strikes. You often learn the hard way. You are a motivating, dynamic leader.

Your worst trait may be your short temper. You can get heated and excited. You do not like to beat around the bush. You are not afraid of risky ventures and will quickly grasp new opportunities. You have a need for speed - in everything! You need to learn to allow time for things to develop. Aries fights offensively by nature, unlike Scorpio whose style is defensive. You attack when necessary. On a personal level you have a strong need to relate to, understand, and be fair to other people.

You enjoy taking on leadership roles, physical challenges, and individual sports. You dislike inactivity, delays, and meaningless tasks.

Aries Fulfillment: You find fulfillment in your career, status, your home, and family. You can use your gift of leadership as a foundation to build your status and career. You must learn to balance your work and home lives as your competitive spirit may cause an imbalance. Through these you will uncover your identity, needs, desires, and gain awareness and confidence.

55

You work well under pressure and your gift of quick mental decisiveness makes your skills perfect in a Mountain of Influence where fast thinking is required, such as paramedic, emergency room nurse or doctor, surgeon, police officer, firefighter, military, salesperson, or in the advertising field where new and different ideas are always needed.

Aries Pride of Life: Being the first Sign of the Zodiac you are #1 and know it. You are proud of yourself and want to make the most of who you are. 'You' are the center of your life.

Keeping Pride in Check: Make the most of each opportunity to learn patience and sacrifice for others. Take time to put yourself in the service of others and periodically follow rather than lead. Learn to reflect on things before taking action. Try not to compare yourself to others.

Aries Challenging/Unbalanced Traits: You can be impulsive, rash, impatient, selfish, short-tempered, domineering, aggressive, too passionate, possessive, or reckless. You do not like to take advice from others and often start but do not finish projects.

Sun in Taurus, April 21 – May 20

TAURUS

TAURUS NATURE: Steady, persistent, reliable, stubborn, patient, practical, and sensual. You are responsible, stable, and devoted.

With your Sun in Taurus you are determined, yet generally patient. Of all the signs you have the most common sense and are good at offering practical advice. You are a good steward of all things under your care and are considered exceptionally reliable. You were born to find comfort and gratification. You can be possessive and keep things for life. You may be a slow learner, but once you grasp something you retain it. You believe in the tangible, concrete matters of the day rather than philosophical or spiritual matters.

You like to be at home in your own environment. You want peace and harmony and stay away from disruptive situations. You tend to be an eternal optimist. Nothing seems to get you upset. However, when pushed to a certain point, you have a strong temper. You enjoy the comforts of the world and can get too comfortable and stagnate, not wanting to change in a given situation. You have artistic and creative talents and enjoy taking time to stop and enjoy life.

Your worst fault could be your stubbornness. You cannot be forced to change your mind and you only see your side of the story. You do not like change, especially when you did not initiate it. You like land and what money can buy including high quality clothes and furniture. The more self-confident you become the more it will be reflected in your possessions.

You like beauty and working with your hands through gardening and cooking. You also enjoy music and romance. You dislike sudden changes, complications, and insecurity of any kind.

Taurus Fulfillment: You find fulfillment through your friends, groups, social events, and the successful result of the efforts you have taken toward your hopes and dreams, as well as through your children, creativity, fun, speculation, and romance. When you learn how to appreciate the beauty and pleasures of your life you will eliminate fear and anger.

Your high integrity, reliability, and financial skills may lead you to work in the Business Mountain through banking, securities, mutual funds, real estate, commerce, or finance.

Your creative talents work well as a hair stylist, interior decorator, musician, or artist. Your sympathetic and stable nature fits well in careers such as doctors, nurses, teachers, and social workers. Your love of nature can draw you into farming, ranching, or the produce industry.

Taurus Pride of Life: You are proud of your possessions and your values. Material things including money can be the center of your life.

Keeping Pride in Check: Make the most of each opportunity to learn to value other philosophies and learn to appreciate the spiritual values of life. Take other people's views into consideration. Learn to be generous and give of yourself and your possessions to your partnerships.

Taurus Challenging/Unbalanced Traits: You can be slow to move and resistant to change. You can be inflexible, reactive, greedy, and self-indulgent. You can be too fearful of change or losing your possessions. You can be stubborn, possessive, and uncompromising.

GEMINI

GEMINI NATURE: Communicative, curious, logical, rational, and gentle. You are dualistic, distractible, versatile, and adaptable.

With your Sun in Gemini you are interested in the world of ideas and were born to be a student of life. You are an instinctive communicator and can easily exchange ideas. You associate well with people and are popular. You are inquisitive and learn quickly. Quickly is the way to describe the way you decide, respond, and change. You go with the flow.

Your mental database is filled with a lot of information. Gemini is the most theoretical of Signs.   You thrive on theory. You can collect information and react to it at the same time. You are a 'jack of all trades master of none' and know a little about a lot of things. You hold your own opinion high. You have diverse interests and multi-task very well.

Your worst trait can be your short attention span. You are very curious and like to ask "Why?" to every answer given. You are a good performer and you do well in trivia games. Being dualistic in nature may make it hard for people to understand you. One time you are charming and the next you are irritable and sarcastic, leaving them wondering. You have high mental energy and crave variety in life. You like to try new things and if you like it you will do it again, and if not, you see no need to.

You like music, books, and magazines, talking with nearly anyone, and short travels. You do not like to focus or spend a lot of time on any one thing for very long.

Gemini Fulfillment: You find fulfillment in spiritual studies and sacrificial service to others. Satisfaction comes from a deeper approach to life. Maintaining a good mental attitude provides you with good physical health and vice versa. You enjoy helping others. You need complete freedom of movement without a dull routine, where each day holds exciting challenges for you.

Your ability to learn and accumulate knowledge may be used in the education Mountain as a teacher, journalist, or writer. Your gift of speaking and quick mind would work well in an occupation such as a salesperson, cable, or television voiceover actor, or in the entertainment field as a comedian, or playwright.

Gemini Pride of Life: You are proud of your own ideas. What you know and communicate is the center of your life.

Keeping Pride in Check: Make the most of each opportunity to learn to experience practical reality and not just theory. Delve into more focused feelings instead of skimming the surface with superficial knowledge. Take a little longer to find the truth. Be more respectful of other people's thoughts.

Gemini Challenging/Unbalanced Traits: You can be nervous, inconsistent, lose focus, and scattered. You can be indecisive, shallow minded or superficial. You like to have the last word.

Sun in Cancer, June 21 - July 22

CANCER

CANCER NATURE: Emotionally sensitive, tenacious, and protective. You are loyal, sympathetic, persuasive, and intuitive.

With your Sun in Cancer the meaning of 'home' carries a lot of emotion with it. You have strong feelings for family. The ancestry and the roots from which you came give you security for your life. You are protective, sensitive, nurturing, mothering, patriotic, shy, and safety oriented. You are sensitive to other people's moods and like to nurture others. You enjoy exchanging feelings and were born to learn to master yours.

Emotional and physical safety are important to you and you seek security in material comforts. The symbol of Cancer is the crab that carries their home on their back. You withdraw into your shell when you get the slightest criticism or rejection from others. You keep your soft side well protected.

Your worst trait is being too clingy. You can be afraid of the future and are reassured by the past and its memories. You do not take a direct approach. You may take three steps forward and one step back in accomplishing your goals, but you find a way to accomplish them. You want to feel like you are making a difference. You have high intuition and must learn to develop your logic and work together with it.

You like one on one conversations, art, home-based hobbies, relaxing near or in the water, helping loved ones or a good meal with friends. You dislike strangers, any criticism of your mother, or revealing your personal life to others.

Cancer Fulfillment: You find fulfillment through developing your personality and having a warm loving home. Your life is nourished by your family heritage. A good spiritual partner or spouse can help you fulfill your life's purpose.

61

Your affinity for home, family and heritage can be used in careers that deal with these areas such as the food industry, real estate, or coin and stamp collecting. Caring for others through the Religious or Healthcare Mountains of medicine, nursing, social and welfare work may be a good use of your gifts of sympathy and sensitivity.

Cancer Pride of Life: You are proud of your home. Your family is the center of your life. You want to keep them all to yourself.

Keeping Pride in Check: Make the most of each opportunity to learn to socialize and be more inclusive of those outside of your family. Learn to come out of your shell by being active in group activities that could benefit you or someone else. Learn to grow from travel experiences, exploring new places, philosophizing, and building a friendship network.

Cancer Challenging/Unbalanced Traits: You can be unwavering, moody, possessive, suspicious, manipulative, or insecure. The fear of being emotionally hurt can keep you immobilized.

Sun in Leo, July 23 - August 22

LEO

LEO NATURE: Creative, generous, passionate, and a leader. You are warm-hearted, cheerful, dramatic, humorous, faithful, and loving.

With your Sun in Leo you are dignified, proud, and honorable. Organization is important to you and you need a sense of order and control in your life. You are honest, warm, and loyal. You are a natural born leader and like to organize and delegate to the other Signs around you. You demand respect and will dismiss anyone who treats you otherwise.

You broadcast your self-assurance to the world. You are strong-willed and seldom ask for help because you do not feel you need it. You were born to seek the spotlight and see others around you in supporting roles. You have a childlike nature and wonder of the world. You take life on in a wholehearted manner. You are the most creative Sign, love fun, and can be dramatic. Leos enjoy thinking about themselves and can be vain if they do not get their ego built in a positive way.

Arrogance can be your worst trait. You need to be loved and admired and told often that you are wonderful. You are affectionate, loving, and generous, and like romance, play, and pleasure. You have a tendency for drama. You can be a good actor and can play your role once you know what it is. You are susceptible to flattery.

You like the theater, taking vacations, being admired, expensive things, bright colors, and fun with friends. You dislike being ignored, facing difficult realities, and not being treated like a king or queen.

Leo Fulfillment: You find fulfilment in material comforts, good values, and your creations which include your children. Your desire for children brings you intimacy. Your gift of being able to

63

birth new ideas provides fulfillment as does being recognized for a job well done.

You have good organizational abilities and a way of handling others under your control with constructive authority. Your talents can be used in supervisory or managerial positions or as a military leader. Your dramatic flair is great for acting and entertainment and you may be drawn to the Political Mountain with your magnetic personality.

Leo Pride of Life: You are enormously proud of yourself and what you create. Your creations are the center of your life.

Keeping Pride in Check: Make the most of each opportunity to learn to think of others instead of yourself. Keep an open mind about others to help overcome self-absorption. Learn to be serious and take responsibility for yourself alone and not just for show. Balance finishing tasks with your attitude of play. Learn to say, "I'm sorry."

Leo Challenging/Unbalanced Traits: You can be arrogant, bossy, and vain, always knowing best, as well as stubborn, self-centered, lazy, inflexible, pompous, pretentious, interfering, and thinking the world is all for you.

Sun in Virgo, August 23 – September 22

VIRGO

VIRGO NATURE: Practical, analytical, service-oriented, and hard working. You are gentle, loyal, kind, and detail oriented.

With your Sun in Virgo you operate and think on a micro level. You are the critical thinker of the Zodiac. You are selective, meticulous, and fastidious. You were born with a continual quest for detail, order, and perfection. You have a lot of energy and need to have an outlet. You prefer to serve and would rather take orders and carry out assignments rather than be the boss. You seldom ask 'why,' only 'how?' Your perfectionism could prevent you from grasping the bigger picture.

Your worst trait is being a chronic fault finder, finding fault in yourself and others. You are handy, modest, kind, and humble. You do not like confrontation or being direct. This can lead to bottled up emotions. You have many hobbies and look forward to retirement when you can spend more time working on them.

You like animals, healthy food, books, nature, and cleanliness. You dislike rudeness, asking for help, or taking center stage.

Virgo Fulfillment: You find fulfillment through knowledge and learning how to fix things, including yourself. Since worry is at the root of most of your problems, you get satisfaction through using your analytical, critical, and practical talents to find solid answers. As you learn to see past your five senses you can be fulfilled through faith and spirituality. You can enjoy good health because of a good mental attitude, thoughts, and philosophy.

You have an excellent capacity for gathering and interpreting knowledge and material. Your talents will do well in Mountains of Influence where accuracy is a must. Your gift of critical thinking can give you the opportunity to become an excellent critic, teacher, bookkeeper, secretary, or data processor. Because of your great

65

capacity to care for others you would make a good healer, nurse, doctor, medical technician, or dietician.

Virgo Pride of Life: You are proud of your perfection. Health and service is the center of your life.

Keeping Pride in Check: Make the most of each opportunity to learn to lead in some area of life. Learn to give advice to others without judgmental motives. Do not assume you know it all. Learn to see life from the macro level of the world instead of the micro level of service.

Virgo Challenging/Unbalanced Traits: You can be an extreme perfectionist. Being too critical can keep you from 'seeing the forest for the trees.' You can be excessively shy, over worry, overly critical of yourself and others, all work and no play. You feel like you must always be helping.

Sun in Libra, September 23 - October 22

LIBRA

LIBRA NATURE: Cooperative, graceful, charming, balanced, diplomatic. You are easy going, creative, idealistic, and enjoy partnership.

With your Sun in Libra you are the natural peacemaker of the Zodiac. You were born to see other people's perspectives. You are fair-minded and sociable. Social skills are particularly important to you as Libra is the most social of all the Sun Signs. You have good manners, are a welcomed guest, and can provide fresh ideas. You are a good sounding board and people confide in you.

You care about everyone and their opinions, and you see both sides of every story. Because of this, making decisions can be difficult for you. Life can be a balancing act where you weigh all your options and have a hard time making up your mind. Indecision may be your worst fault.

Partnership and marriage are especially important to you and there can be increasing success after marriage. Companionship is foremost in your mind and you are miserable when alone. You are concerned with equality, compromise, symmetry, and peace. You can be persuasive, civil, courteous, and elegant.

You have a hard time leaving well enough alone and can turn the simplest problems into a complication. You can be a good leader, but you do not feel comfortable doing business if everyone does not win. You do not want anyone to get hurt.

You like companionship, commitment, harmony, sharing with others, and the outdoors. You dislike violence, injustice, loudmouths, and unconformity.

Libra Fulfillment: You find fulfillment in having a good spouse. Marriage gives you the opportunity for a good family life. Your genetics, heritage, and parents help to build your identity. The

67

foundation of partnership helps you to fulfill your destiny as you realize that success with others is more important than success alone.

You have a sense of justice which is needed in areas where fairness is needed such as the Legal Mountain in roles including attorneys, judges, or court reporters. Your artistic talent can lead to careers dealing with music, singing, dancing, the stage, or television. You may also deal with luxury items, cosmetics, hair styling, and interior decorating. You can have attractive features that can lend themselves to the modeling industry. You may be excellent at public relations or as a diplomat. Marriage counselling is an occupation that may interest you.

Libra Pride of Life: You are proud of your partner and relationships. Other people are the center of your life.

Keeping Pride in Check: Make the most of each opportunity to learn to make practical business type decisions instead of the ones where you are always being overly fair or trying to make everyone happy. Endeavor to overcome the fear of failure. Learn how to be comfortable alone at times and think about your own opinions to understand who you are.

Libra Challenging/Unbalanced Traits: You can be vacillating, indecisive, a people pleaser, avoid confrontations, carry a grudge, and have self-pity. You can be gullible, uncertain, and worry too much about what others think. You fear making a bad choice.

Sun in Scorpio, October 23 - November 21

SCORPIO

SCORPIO NATURE: Secretive, intense, controlling, resourceful, and a long-term true friend. You are forceful, magnetic, and brave.

With the Sun in Scorpio you have deep emotions and desires. Scorpio is the most intense Sign of the Zodiac. You were born to search for deep truth even if it involves issues which are taboo. Scorpios are the private eyes, detectives, scientific and spiritual researchers of the Zodiac. You like truth, facts, and getting to the heart of the matter.

You have a keen sense of purpose and will work hard to achieve your goals. You are driven, focused, passionate, sexy, deep, a survivor, are self-controlled, penetrating, and potent. Your energy can seem overpowering and you may intimidate others. Unlike the Sun Sign of Aries, which fights offensively, those born under Scorpio fight defensively. Scorpios carefully plan their defense moves, laying out traps and waiting patiently for the right moment to settle the score. Scorpios never forget a slight.

Your inability to trust people may be your worst trait. You need total commitment from those with whom you are close. You do not feel comfortable unless you are in control and have the upper hand. You are good in a crisis.

You like being right and having longtime friends. You dislike dishonesty, revealing your secrets, and passive people.

Scorpio Fulfillment: You find fulfillment through developing your deep creativity with the goal of delivering results. This comes through passionate involvement with groups, causes, and friendships in order to bring forth growth and transformation. As you become more empathetic and consider people for their worth as humans, and not their material value, your relationships will deepen.

69

You may have a gift and love of healing and can make an excellent doctor, health care worker, nurse, dentist, or surgeon. Research is second nature and can be used in the Mountains of Influence that deal with engineering, mechanics, metaphysics, Astrology, and other spiritual sciences. You may work in fields that deal with other people's money such as payroll, mortgages, insurance, or wills.

Scorpio Pride of Life: You are proud of your standard of living and your power. Control is the center of your life.

Keeping Pride in Check: Make the most of each opportunity to learn to see the importance of lighter, less emotional, more superficial meanings of life rather than only the deep and mysterious ones. Learn to play fair. Learn to truly share with others instead of using what you share to gain control.

Scorpio Challenging/Unbalanced Traits: You can carry a grudge, be traumatic, unforgiving, jealous, and intimidating. You can be overly suspicious and revengeful to those who have betrayed you. You can be distrusting, jealous, secretive, angry, obsessive, compulsive, and possessive.

Sun in Sagittarius,
November 22 - December 21

SAGITTARIUS

SAGITTARIUS NATURE: Freedom loving, truth-seeker, straight-forward, broadminded, philosophical, idealistic, and an explorer. You are generous, honest, have a great sense of humor, and like to travel. You look for happy endings.

With your Sun in Sagittarius you are the explorers of the Zodiac and seek adventure. You search out faraway places, whether it be material, physical or spiritual. You were born to explore the heights of spiritual, religious, and philosophical truth. You have strong faith, are forgiving, loving, and ethical. You do not hold grudges.

You enjoy philosophy, multicultural experiences and seek for new horizons with a positive spirit. Money may not be as important to you as spiritual principles and pursuits. You give things away thinking others need it more than you. You are critical of your own behavior and take full responsibility for your actions. You learn from your mistakes.

If you want to know what someone thinks, ask a Sagittarius! You speak the truth but can be blunt and this can be your worst trait. At times you speak before you think, and it upset others. Sagittarius needs a challenge and enjoys achieving. As soon as one challenge is finished, you start on the next one. You seek pleasure at any cost and may be irresponsible and reckless in your behavior. You are curious and love to travel. You can be hard to pin down. Restlessness can be a severe problem. You need to feel the pressure to succeed. You are outgoing, optimistic, and upwardly mobile.

You like freedom and being outdoors. You would like to travel around the world. Sagittarius dislikes clingy people, being constrained, off-the-wall theories, and details.

71

Sagittarius Fulfillment: You find fulfillment through serving other people. You help other people improve their lives by sharing your wisdom and revealing truths through the insights you have learned. Your responsibilities and obligations are opportunities to solidify your own opinions. Religion and spiritual practices give structure to your need for higher learning.

Your can do well in places of Higher Education, Religious, or Spiritual Mountains as you have an expansive mind and like to undertake new studies. The legal and judicial system would be a natural place for you to make use of your desire to seek truth. Employment related to travel or the import-export business may interest you. You can use your gifts and talents in the Mountains of Influence that deal with mass communications, radio, internet, cable, literature and all published material, as well as fields that require keeping up to date with happenings around the world. Lecturing and living in distant places is possible.

Sagittarius Pride of Life: You are proud of your fearlessness. Your own philosophies are the center of your life.

Keeping Pride in Check: Make the most of each opportunity to spend time learning about the roots and foundation of subjects instead of always focusing on the esoteric. Challenge yourself to find opportunities for enjoyment in the practical realm instead of only in the spiritual. Keep your spiritual craving in balance by working on activities that are material and keep you involved in the physical.

Sagittarius Unbalanced/Challenging Traits: You can be tactless and awkward in your speech and mannerisms. You can have blind optimism, often promising more than you can deliver. You do not always see projects through. You are impatient and will say what you think no matter how undiplomatic it may be.

CAPRICORN

CAPRICORN NATURE: Achiever, reserved, mature, and disciplined. You are conservative, responsible, determined, self-controlled, grounded, and concerned with status.

With your Sun in Capricorn you are ambitious and are empowered by authority, structure, and tradition. Capricorn is the most mature and serious Sun Sign of the Zodiac. You were born to work hard and earn respect. You are old for your age when you are young and young for your age when you get older! Capricorn generally has a difficult childhood that improves with age. You are a loner and are slow to make friends. You have a dry sense of humor.

You are self-directed and have a drive to succeed. Success is a requisite for your self-worth. You are dedicated and trustworthy and need approval from those in authority. You make and follow your own boundaries, come up with your own game plan and refine it until it works. You are hardworking and keep to the task until the goal is achieved.

Being condescending can be your worst trait. You demand a lot from yourself and others. It can be hard for others to meet your standards. You have a hard time being carefree and always want to be working on serious matters. Time and money are important. You like to learn everything through actual experience and practice. You are persistent, ambitious, and reliable.

You like status, quality craftsmanship, rank, and concrete results. You dislike just about everything at some point in your life.

Capricorn Fulfillment: You find fulfillment and security through your career, home, and family. You seek a worthy cause and the status that attracts a good partner, who will help you build your

73

home and career as you fulfill your destiny. The more you share your talents with the world the more accomplished you will feel.

You appreciate authority and order and prefer the executive side of your careers. You are a doer, achiever, goal-oriented which makes you suited for entrepreneurial type businesses. There is the tendency toward authoritarianism, bureaucracy, and insensitivity in business dealings.

You understand the process of building and know how to rise to the top in your career. You do well in the Mountains of Influence that involve large building and business schemes and will generally see them through. You will be seen as a leader, executive, and authority in whatever occupation you choose.

Capricorn Pride of Life: You are proud of your achievements, success, and authority. Power and status are the center of your life.

Keeping Pride in Check: Make the most of each opportunity to learn how to play and enjoy life. Relinquish control at times. Learn how to see things theoretically and spiritually rather than solely from material experience. Give credence to other people's abilities. Realize that everything that you have acquired is not from your merit but a gift from God. Enjoy the moment instead of always planning for the future.

Capricorn Unbalanced/Challenging Traits: You can be too conservative, miserly, and gloomy. You can suffer from inhibition, lack of self-confidence, and pessimism. You can be unforgiving, condescending, expect the worst, and avoid true connections with others. You can take too long to prepare before starting a project.

AQUARIUS

AQUARIUS NATURE: Independent, original, unique, and progressive. You are individualistic, contrary, humanitarian, futuristic, stubborn, and socially aware, yet somewhat traditional.

With your Sun in Aquarius you embody the unity of man and all types of humanitarian or humane objectives. You are a friendly, freedom-oriented Sign, yet are very private and aloof. You are born to work for humanitarian causes with the goal of changing the world in a big way. This involves collaborating with groups of people to work towards breaking down existing structures. You try to surround yourself with people and circumstances that are in alignment with the positive changes you want to make.

Your worst trait can be your fear of emotional attachment. You understand people very well. Even so, you want to keep your distance from others. You are a good listener. You are objective, unconventional and can engage in activism. You are a rebel with a cause. As you learn new ways of living, you pass the information along to others. You set yourself apart from the crowd by your originality.

You like fun with friends, helping others, fighting for worthwhile causes, and intellectual conversations. You dislike limitations, broken promises, being lonely, dull, or boring situations, and people who disagree with you.

Aquarius Fulfillment: You find fulfilment by finding ways to take care of the needs of all humanity while making valuable connections with others as a whole. You need one good close relationship that encourages you to express love while at the same time allowing you to be emotionally detached enough to fulfill your humanitarian efforts.

75

As an Aquarius you have a high degree of intelligence with even occasional sparks of genius. These talents are suitable in Mountains of Influence involving teaching, research, science, inventing, lecturing, writing, technical fields, music, composing, voiceover artist, and journalism. You have a strong interest in careers that have a futuristic, technological, or spiritual focus. You are suited for a humanitarian career that promotes beliefs and undertakings which are not always orthodox or accepted by the general public.

Aquarius Pride of Life: You are proud of your individuality and the rewards you receive from your humanitarian career. Helping humanity is the center of your life.

Keeping Pride in Check: Make the most of each opportunity to help individual people instead of only the group as a whole. Learn how to stay focused in an area of committed service to help you overcome threats to your freedom. Learn the reward of service and longer-term commitment to others. Learn about the old in order to build the new on a solid foundation.

Aquarius Unbalanced/Challenging Traits: You can be detached, willful and often agitated. You can be temperamental, contrary, unpredictable, uncompromising, egotistical, radical, unable to commit, aloof, and fear the loss of your freedom. You may be unwilling to accept other's opinions.

PISCES

PISCES NATURE: Compassionate, idealistic, dreamer, and creative. You are artistic, intuitive, gentle, kind, wise, self-sacrificing, and unworldly.

With your Sun in Pisces you were born with an amazing ability to get along with others and give unconditional love. Pisces is known to have the smallest of all egos in the Zodiac. You do not like to worry about yourself, instead you care for others. It is one of your strongest attributes. You can be the best of all friends and people feel comfortable confiding in you. Pisces is the least social of all signs and is introverted and private.

You are spiritually and intuitively sensitive and reach beyond what is tangible. Because of this sensitivity, you can be easily hurt and therefore want to escape and live in a world of fantasy. You need some time each day to get away from it all and be alone to recharge. You work selflessly in the background. You can be so busy doing for others that you do not reach for your own highest potential. You often provide the backdrop to life events as you like to join with others and do not want to stand out in the crowd.

Trusting others too easily can be your worst fault and can lead to being taken advantage of. You are sacrificial, understanding, ambiguous, spiritual, wise, and devoted. Your creativity can draw you to glamor, designing and making beautiful clothes. You can learn to rely on unhealthy habits and are given to excesses. You are a hopeless romantic.

You like being alone, sleeping, music, romance, fantasy, and spiritual themes. You dislike being criticized, cruelty of any kind, and being stuck in the past.

Pisces Fulfillment: You find fulfillment through deep spirituality and religion. The suffering experienced from self-sacrifice fulfills itself in spirituality. You fulfill your life through your gift of faith and tireless service toward others. You are aware of the suffering of others and can help others through a caring or spiritual type of profession.

Pisces can find inner peace ministering within the walls of large institutions such as nursing homes, churches, hospitals, halfway houses, jails, or prisons. You have a quick comprehensive, intelligent mind with good judgment and the ability to do many things. Your talents can be used in Mountains of Influence involved with musical and artistic endeavors, photography, publicity, advertising, chemistry, anesthesia, hospitals, film acting, and singing.

Pisces Pride of Life: You are proud of your faith. Caring for others, self-sacrifice, and privacy are the center of your life.

Keeping Pride in Check: Make the most of each opportunity to learn how to open up emotionally in your partnerships. Learn to keep a healthy balance between humility and a healthy need to protect yourself. At times you need to find things to do for yourself.

Pisces Challenging/Unbalanced Traits: You can be idealistic, vague, weak-willed, aimless, lost, disillusioned, escapist, and elusive. You can become a victim or martyr or lose your identity as you naturally blend with others.

The Moon,
Reflecting the Light of the Sun

*And God made the two great lights.... **and the lesser light to rule the night**... Genesis 1:16 ESV*

Astrology as practiced by our Spiritual Forefathers, used both the Sun and Moon (as well as the Rising Sign) to understand their Natal Charts (Mazal) and their place in God's world. Today we still use these three Luminaries when we construct a Natal Chart. They make up your Primary Star Pattern.

While your Sun Sign describes your core personality, the Moon Sign represents your emotions, moods, and your more intimate side. The Sun, the ruler of the day, represents where you shine. The Moon, as ruler of the night represents how you 'reflect' the sunshine.

The Moon represents the less obvious activity of your life, your deepest emotions, and your feeling nature. It describes how you instinctively respond or react to the events in your life and the environment around you.

The Moon is nurturing and governs the urge to protect yourself. It reveals your emotional responses and habits. The Moon suggests how you are likely to make decisions about matters that affect your physical and emotional safety.

In a Hebraic and Messianic understanding, the Moon has come to be known as representing God's people, spiritual Israel. The Moon projects the light of the Sun upon the Earth at night. Spiritual Israel projects God's light and His Good News to this dark world. Born-again Believers are to project this light into a dark world, too. (Matthew 16:15) In a spiritual way, the Moon represents our soul, as we reflect the light of God in our lives.

As your Moon influences your emotional and more intimate side it reveals:

- Your inner desires, emotions, and memories
- All that you internalize and keep from others
- The mother/maternal energy in your Chart
- Your immediate emotional response to life's situations
- Your instinctive nature
- The part of you that is hidden but often comes out
  in highly stressful situations

By knowing which Sign your Moon is in, you can also understand:

- How you nurture others
- How you like to be nurtured
- How you meet your physical and emotional needs
- How you react in emotional situations
- How you process emotions
- How you protect yourself

Your Moon Sign

Just as your Sun was in a certain Zodiac Sign at your birth, so the Moon was in a certain Sign also. The Moon travels through each of the twelve Zodiac signs each Month and therefore its Sign changes frequently throughout the Month. An Ephemeris will show you where the Moon was at the time of your birth. Casting a computerized Natal Chart will also show you.

The Moon Sign often shows the area of life that gives you the most comfort and security. It can also show how you retreat when you need rest, quiet or refuge. It can describe the type of emotional nurturing you received from your parent or primary caregiver. Lastly it can reveal details of your domestic life.

The Moon indicates the processes you use in your daily activities. We have one type of individuality, indicated by the Sun, and often a quite different method for accomplishing our goals, indicated by the Moon.

The Moon indicates how your nature, as shown by the Sun, will be developed in your life. It works with the Sun to fulfill your life purpose. The qualities of your Moon Sign help you to accomplish your life goals set by the purpose of your Sun.

Once you find the Sign your Moon occupies, you can identify its qualities and will be able to distinguish them from your Sun's qualities. You can mentally compartmentalize which qualities go with each Luminary in order to understand their separate functions. You will be able to see what they have in common, where they complement one another, and where they differ. Your entire emotional mode of operation is dictated by a combination of both the Sun Sign and the Moon Sign.

By considering the Sun and Moon together as a team and looking at just these two points in the Chart, you can learn much about how you fulfill your desires and needs. The Sun and its Sign give you goals and direction that inspire your life. The Moon's characteristics work to fulfill the needs and desires of your heart, your Sun. They work together to accomplish their individual roles.

Your Moon Sign plays an important part in how strongly your Sun Sign can express itself. You can have a fiery Aries Sun but have a practical Virgo Moon, which means you would have some fast-paced and aggressive goals that are toned down by the practical, slower moving instincts of Virgo. Or vice versa, you can have a practical Sun in Virgo and your Moon in Aries. Your emotions will want to express themselves quickly and directly, and they may be forced to tone down because of the Virgo practicality. This may be a good brake for you so you do not spout off, or it may be a cause of frustration, not being able to express yourself freely. These are some examples of how the Sun and Moon can affect one another.

The Rising Sign, which we will learn about in a later chapter, is also part of this harmonious work. This harmony of the Luminaries works throughout your life to help accomplish your purpose. Let us look at each of the Zodiac signs as they pertain to the Moon.

The Moon in Each Zodiac Sign

(The Astrological symbol for the Zodiac Sign is shown with its Moon Sign title.)

♈

Moon in Aries

The Moon in Aries indicates you have a strong need for action and become easily bored. Your moods and emotions are extremely quick to surface. You are a fast driver and have an excellent reaction to danger.

You are incredibly determined and want to follow your own path of action, right or wrong. You do not like interference from others. You have sudden flare ups of temper, but they are quickly forgotten. You are prone to taking the reactions of others personally. You can lose patience with those slower than yourself, only to regret it later.

You act on your feelings and instincts. You instinctively put yourself first. If you can control your impulsive tendencies, you can be very decisive. You encourage others to do things themselves.

The Moon in Aries' best traits are your sense of optimism and drive, and your worst traits are your impatience and temper.

Your emotional responses are impulsive. You protect yourself by taking charge and lashing out.

83

Moon in Taurus

The Moon in Taurus indicates a strong need for material security. You display common sense in handling financial and home affairs. Your moods and emotions tend to be steady and serene. Negative emotional reactions lead to overindulgences such as overeating, overspending, or being lazy.

You can develop an excess attachment to material things. Possessiveness and stubbornness are challenging traits that need to be overcome. You need a nudge to start new projects, but once they are started, you will see them though.

This position of the Moon generally attracts wealth and a good life. You surround yourself with the beautiful comfortable things of life. A stable home life is important to your emotional security. You adhere to conservative and conventional principles.

The Moon in Taurus' best trait is your loyalty and your worst traits are being stubborn and overly self-indulgent.

Your emotional responses are deep and strong. You protect yourself with your material possessions.

♊

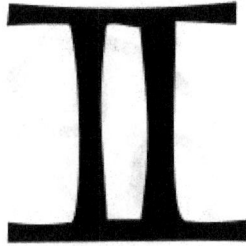

Moon in Gemini

The Moon in Gemini indicates a strong need to communicate with the world. A quick verbal response is characteristic. You tend to talk incessantly. Your moods and emotions are dualistic. One minute you respond one way and the next your response is another way. You rationalize your emotions and have a hard time trusting them. Sometimes you are not sure of how you really feel.

You are a great multi-tasker and can start several tasks at one time but may have trouble bringing them through to completion. You are resourceful in coming up with solutions. You are very curious and like to ask many questions. You are an interesting companion and guest with a broad range of interests and skills. You need an outlet for your tremendous resource of energy. If it stagnates or slows down you become impatient, restless, and are filled with nervous energy.

The Moon in Gemini's best traits are your enthusiastic and curious nature, and your worst traits are that you can be deceitful and gossipy.

Your emotional responses are changeable. You protect yourself with what you know and by rationalizing your emotions.

Moon in Cancer

The Moon in Cancer indicates a strong need for emotional security. Your moods and emotions are strong, self-protective, and changeable. You feel things very deeply. You feel first, then you think about it. You can go from joy to sadness to anger and back again within seconds. You are extremely sensitive to the moods and feelings of others. This can sometimes lead to imagined slights, which can lead to many tears.

You have strong intuition and instincts and you should learn how to use them. Domestic relationships are important. There can be a strong tie to your mother. You may be a good cook. You can be an overly concerned parent, always worrying and imagining the worst. Security is especially important to you and may lead to hoarding and secretiveness. A secure home environment is important to your emotional safety.

The Moon in Cancer's best traits are your maternal and caring nature, and your worst trait is being overly emotional.

Your first emotional response is defensiveness. You protect yourself by retreating and hiding in your shell.

Moon in Leo

The Moon in Leo indicates a strong need to be admired and appreciated. Your moods and emotions are proud. You enjoy the spotlight and have a dramatic flair. You need to love and be loved and need romance and affection. You can be self-centered, egotistical, and stubborn. You may hide your lack of self-confidence and self-esteem by bragging and vanity. You like mixing and surrounding yourself with the finer things of life and those who flatter you. This could lead to snobbishness.

You cope well in any emergency because your leadership and organizational ability can be expressed at a moment's notice. Your immediate instinct is to take over. It is easy for you to appear bossy, dogmatic, and stubborn. You believe that you can do anything as well or better than anyone else. You have great potential, can be a high achiever, and an inspiration to others. You hate to admit you are wrong. If you ever do admit it, you are serious about it.

The Moon in Leo's best trait is your charisma, and your worst traits are your pride and vanity.

Your emotional response is to take charge. You protect yourself with your ego, pride, and vanity.

♍

Moon in Virgo

The Moon in Virgo indicates a strong desire to categorize and organize your needs and habits. Your moods and emotions are rational. You have an extremely hard working and practical nature. You do things well and like to figure things out. You can be talkative when nervous or challenged.

You are concerned with neatness and cleanliness for yourself and your household. You are particular about food, diet, and health. You are detail oriented and can have a critical spirit. You have good literary skills.

You can have quick reactions, have good common sense, and are extremely practical in your approach, leaving the emotional consideration to others. You may become too predictable. You are considerate in your work and personal relationships. You are shy, gentle, and affectionate.

The Moon in Virgo's best trait is being talented at virtually everything, and your worst traits are worry and lack of confidence.

Your emotional responses are practical and efficient. You protect yourself by fixing yourself and your surroundings and keeping everything in order.

Moon in Libra

The Moon in Libra indicates a strong need for harmony and balance in everything you do. Your moods and emotions are fair and agreeable. You are a natural peacemaker and have a great ability to identify with other people's problems and points of view. This can cause you to be indecisive, especially with answers to your own problems. There is an immediate response to others and a willingness to listen. You are instinctively drawn to relationships and partnerships to help provide balance.

Seeing many different points of view can cause you to be unsure of choosing the correct answer. You can become dependent on your partner making decisions for you. You need to balance your needs and instincts. Your emotional wellbeing depends on the approval of others, so you are gracious and courteous. You have an immediate charm and can bring out the best in others. You need to be careful not to be too dependent on others for emotional security.

The Moon in Libra's best traits are your sense of balance and fairness, and your worst trait is indecisiveness.

Your emotional responses are fair and agreeable. You protect yourself through the security of a partner.

♏︎

Moon in Scorpio

The Moon in Scorpio indicates a strong need for power and transformation. Your moods and emotions are strong and are based on conscious desires. Your feelings are easily aroused when you are challenged, and you instinctively overreact when provoked. Outbursts are not uncommon. You want to dominate others through subtle means. Your deep and stubborn emotions can lead to intense situations. You do not forget personal affronts. Jealousy, revenge, possessiveness, and resentment are powerful responses that need to be dealt with.

As the Moon nature is internal, you likely present yourself very differently in the outward displays of your personality. You are instinctively secretive and have covert motives for your actions. Your personality undergoes transformations throughout your life, with your strength and energy being renewed each time.

The Moon in Scorpio's best trait is your passion and your worst trait is the intensity of your emotions.

Your emotional responses are deep and penetrating. You protect yourself by knowing you have a plan of defense available if needed.

Moon in Sagittarius

The Moon in Sagittarius indicates a strong need for freedom and forward motion, both physically and intellectually. Your moods and emotions are positive and enthusiastic. However, you can be blunt and frank in your expression. You have high goals that may lack a sense of reality. You are moody, even unpredictable in your desires. One part of your behavior relies on a constant stream of a moral code that guides your decisions, and another part of you that does whatever it wants without any concern for others. When these two parts do not join together, you scatter your energies and accomplish little.

You seem to not worry too much about details. You are instinctively drawn to distant places and enjoy foreign foods. You have a need to be challenged through risks. When presented with one you rise to the occasion. You search for truth. You can have a strong attachment or response to the religion or philosophy taught to you by your parents in your early childhood.

The Moon in Sagittarius' best trait is your adventurous nature and your worst trait is your restlessness.

Your emotional responses are optimistic and idealistic. You protect yourself by knowing the truth and having faith in higher matters.

Moon in Capricorn

The Moon in Capricorn indicates a strong need for self-preservation. Your moods and emotions are reserved, and you take only carefully calculated risks. You are happiest when you have a goal and are working to achieve it. You take life seriously and identify emotionally with material rather than spiritual values.

You have a very cool, calm reaction to situations and your emotions are rather low and under control. You have a hard time showing emotions and giving or receiving love. You seem detached as if you want to distance yourself from others but in reality, you need a lot of love, affection, and reassurance from others, more so than any other Sign. You have a dry sense of humor and can use it to offset this distance. You can easily become discouraged and need someone to inspire you. You can be shy and unsure about your self-worth. You seek status and financial security for yourself and your family. You are hardworking and ambitious desiring to succeed.

The Moon in Capricorn's best traits are your ambition and resourcefulness, and your worst traits are being cold and condescending.

Your emotional responses are cold and serious. You protect yourself through your solid reputation as well as closing off your emotions.

92

Moon in Aquarius

The Moon in Aquarius indicates a strong need for independence, originality, and emotional detachment. Your moods and emotions are unpredictable and detached. You are friendly to all in an impersonal way. Emotional attachment threatens your personal freedom. While you do have an emotional barrier, when someone breaks through, they see your characteristic kindness. You have a great capacity to sympathize with the needs of humanity. You are very observant of people and life, and notice everything, including the emotional tone of the situation.

You offer help to others and take pleasure in making the offer and not in what you get in return. Your feeling nature is strongly associated with your mental nature, which is mature and self-controlled. You tend to run from emotional attachment and expression. You can have sudden inspirations and solutions. You can be controversial and rebellious and need the freedom to come and go as you please. You may have unusual family relationships.

The Moon in Aquarius' best trait is your concern for all humanity and your worst traits are your fear of emotional intimacy and attachment.

Your emotional response is kind yet distant. You protect yourself by detaching from people. Keeping your emotional distance from others keeps you safe.

93

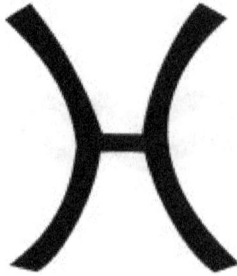

Moon in Pisces

The Moon in Pisces indicates a strong need for sensitivity and imagination. Your moods and emotions are easily moved to great happiness or sadness. You are kind and sympathetic to the feelings of others. You soak up the thoughts and emotions of others and respond by doing something kind and charitable, even to the point of self-denial. Because of your emotional vulnerability you can be hurt easily and can develop a persecution complex and then withdraw. You need time each day to go into seclusion to recharge your emotional batteries. Giving in to any form of negative escapism can become a habit that is hard to break.

You take the road of least resistance. You need to devise a way for you to hold your ground. You need to be sensitive to the intricacies of your needs and instincts and take direct action to express them. Try to be a bit braver in expressing your own feelings so there can be an emotional environment that is mutually supportive and not one-sided.

The Moon in Pisces' best traits are your imagination and creativity, and your worst trait is your over-sensitivity.

Your emotional responses are sensitive and compassionate. You protect yourself by escaping to your own fantasies where the outside world goes away.

The Stars,
Your Face to the World

*And God made the two great lights—the greater light to rule the
day and the lesser light to rule the night—**and the Stars**.*
Genesis 1:16 ESV

The Stars and Your Rising Sign

The Rising Sign is part of the Primary Star Pattern which also
includes the Sun and the Moon. Your Rising Sign is not a Planet
like the Sun and Moon. It is a point identified by the constellation
of Stars that were shining on the Eastern horizon at the moment
of your birth. Depending on its Element and Mode your Rising
Sign will reveal the persona you display to the world and the
mannerisms you use to project and protect yourself throughout
your life.

According to the Ancient Astrology taught from the Biblical
perspective, the Rising Sign is the most important Luminary in
determining how we see life and how others see us. It is described
as the 'Helm' of life. It is the point that sets the position of the
entire Chart and is most personal to us.

Your Rising Sign, also called the Ascendant, sets the tone of your
entire Chart. It is like a veil, or a mask, that you wear as you
interact with the world. It is not something you hide behind,
instead, it represents how you present yourself, both through your
bodily appearance and your personality.

Your Rising Sign colors the way you perceive the world, and it
colors the way other people see and relate to you. It is what people
see when they first meet you. When they get to know you better,
they see the other components of your personality as shown in
your Chart like the Sun and Moon characteristics. Your Rising
Sign reveals the ease and ability with which you must interact with
the outside world.

The Rising Sign is the point on the horizon which alone determines the First House of your Natal Chart. The Houses, which describe the areas of our lives, will be covered in more depth later in this book. For now, you can think of the Rising Sign in the First House like a door that you open and close to the world. How you open and close the door is described by the Zodiac Sign that is in the First House.

The First House is the House of your personality and it represents your social self. It is your physical body and outward style. It determines the facets of yourself that you show to the world.

Your Rising Sign indicates what you want to be known for. The way in which you do this is based on the characteristics of the Zodiac Sign in which it resides. The energies of your Rising Sign set the tone for your entire Chart and work in conjunction with your Sun and Moon.

The position of the Rising Sign in your Natal Chart is very time specific. Some people do not know the exact time of their birth due to lack of access to their detailed birth information. It is not something you can guess at. The position of the constellation, or the Stars, that is rising changes every 4 minutes due to the Earth's rotation. It is easily calculated with Astrology computer programs. Until you know your birth time, you can continue to study your Sun Sign which we have previously covered in this book. The Sun Sign will give you a tremendous amount of information for you to begin to know yourself.

From the rising of the Sun to the place where it sets, the name of the LORD is to be praised. Psalm 113:3

What Makes Up A Rising Sign?

The descriptions of each of the Rising Signs in this section include the more technical components that make up each of the Zodiac Signs. Each Zodiac Sign has several parts that form the basis of its unique characteristics. These parts are listed here so you can see the unique combination that each Sign contains and how they are revealed in your personality.

The components of the Rising Sign's constellation include the following:

Zodiac Sign Symbol – The Symbol of the Rising Sign's constellation
Defining Phrase – The Key Declaration(s) projected by the Rising Sign
Modality* – The Mode of Operation - Cardinal, Fixed, Mutable
Element* – The Element of Matter - Fire, Earth, Air, Water
Polarity* - The Polarizing Energy - Masculine/Feminine, Positive/Negative
Ruling Planet* – The Name of the Planet whose influence drives the direction of the Rising Sign, along with its traditional role nickname
What You Want to be known for – The general motivation of life indicated by the traits of the Rising Sign

Combining these qualities gives each Rising Sign its own unique fundamental characteristics. These are the qualities you have available to work with to achieve your goals, express your emotions, and develop your gifts and talents.

*Detailed descriptions of each of these components can be found in later chapters.

ARIES Rising

Mode: Cardinal
Element: Fire
Polarity: Masculine
Ruling Planet: Mars
Symbol: The Ram

Aries Key declaration: I AM

Those born with Aries Rising are perceived to be naturally ambitious and courageous, and their appearance can be prominent. Aries Rising wants to be known for taking action and their leadership role in starting projects.

You are bold and passionate and want to be first. Aries is both a Cardinal and a Fire Sign which means you have double the powerful initiative and ambition for the promotion of your goals and self-focused interests as well as the energy and enthusiasm to achieve them.

Aries is of the Masculine polarity which indicates outgoingness. Aries' ruling Planet is Mars the 'Warrior' which provides you with the drive, aggression, and competitiveness to act.

The symbol for Aries is the Ram. You are assertive and enterprising. You will ram through anyone who tries to block your efforts.

Aries is the natural Sign of the First House of self, life, and beginnings. With Aries in the First House it is natural for you to be more concerned about your own personal affairs than those of others. You are 'me first' in your desire to develop your personality and appearance in order to live up to your potential.

The opinions of others can easily be second to yours. You have a strong feeling of being in competition with everyone, including yourself. You often feel like you are inferior to others and feel like you have missed many opportunities. Because of this you may have a hard time finding peace of mind.

With Aries Rising you were born with a strong independence and will learn to work with others through the give and take of your close partnerships and relationships.

TAURUS Rising

Quality: Fixed
Element: Earth
Polarity: Feminine
Ruling Planet: Venus
Symbol: The Bull

Taurus Key Declarations: I HAVE, I POSSESS

Those born with Taurus Rising are seen as being reliable and thorough in all their activities. Taurus Rising wants to be known for building up their resources, possessions, and values in a practical steadfast way. You are sensual and passionate and enjoy comfort. You also have the ability to instinctively know the needs of those you love.

Taurus is a Fixed Sign indicating you are stubborn, determined and goal oriented. Taurus is an Earth Element, which indicates you are practical and dependable. The Taurus polarity is Feminine which indicates you are receptive and passive.

The ruling Planet is Venus, the 'Lover,' who represents the motivation to relate and acquire. Your basic impulse is acquisition. You have great potential for accumulating resources. You tend to be materialistic in order to protect yourself. If unbalanced, you can become a pack rat holding on to all your possessions.

The Symbol for Taurus is the Bull. Once a goal is set you have strength of purpose to see it through to the very end. You can be extremely stubborn and have a hard time seeing anyone else's point of view.

Taurus is the natural Sign of the Second House which emphasizes creature comforts, finances, and possessions. It is only natural that you are concerned with your security and personal welfare.

101

Money is meaningful to you. You are a stabilizer who gathers, assimilates, collects, and builds.

You are practical and are concerned with the basic needs of physical life, such as food, shelter, love, and the money to buy what you need. What you need is determined by your individual personal values and whether they are practical or lavish. Taurus is the Sign of value, both material and personal.

With Taurus Rising you were born with a fixed stability and will learn how to transform, change, and share through interactions in your close relationships.

GEMINI Rising

Quality: Mutable
Element: Air
Polarity: Masculine
Ruling Planet: Mercury
Symbol: The Twins

Gemini Key Declarations: I Think, I Communicate

Those born with Gemini Rising are perceived to have two different faces to their personality. Gemini Rising wants to be known for their ability to communicate and exchanging a variety of ideas.

Gemini's mode is Mutable meaning you are flexible and dexterous and can adapt yourself to the needs of others. Gemini's Element is Air indicating that you are intellectual. You have an adaptable mind but will question every concept until it is proven.

You have a Masculine polarity and are confident and outgoing. Gemini's ruling Planet is Mercury the 'Messenger.' You need to communicate.

The symbol for Gemini is the Twins and this represents your dual nature. You thrive on change. You have two sides to your personality. One which is cheerful, flexible, and versatile, fitting into a group. The other is cutting, specific, particular, exploring individual interests.

Gemini is the natural Sign of the Third House which relates to communication, short distance travel, siblings, and neighbors. You need to express yourself and want to go places. You connect with others through your communication skills whether spoken or written, and sometimes both. Your ability to understand conflicting ideas makes you popular. You do not want to deal with jealousy or possessiveness. You have a great independent streak. You can have several projects going on all at once.

You cultivate a wide variety of interests making you a fine teacher because of the richness of information you possess and your ability to recall it. It will be beneficial to learn to focus and prioritize your multiple interests in order to get things done.

With Gemini Rising you were born with the need for diversity and will learn the value of consistency through your partnerships.

CANCER Rising

Quality: Cardinal
Element: Water
Polarity: Feminine
Ruling Planet: The Moon
Symbol: The Crab

Cancer Key Declarations: I Feel, I Nurture

Those born with Cancer Rising are seen as someone whose focus is on home and family. Cancer Rising wants to be known for creating and sustaining emotional bonds with those to whom they are close.

Cancer is a Cardinal Sign and you initiate action to preserve your inner security and protect your home and family. You are a leader but will often lead from behind. You are steady in a crisis and are tenacious in getting what you want.

Cancer is a Water Sign which colors your nature with strong emotional sensitivity and spiritual or intuitive ability. You love to care for others and tend to form a close circle of friends that is closed to others. You are concerned with safety. You have a receptive, Feminine polarity and are a nurturer, offering support and sympathy when needed.

The ruling Planet for Cancer Rising is the Moon, which is not a Planet, but the natural satellite of the Earth. The Moon represents responsiveness, sensitivity, and nurturing as well as fluctuating moods. The Moon goes through phases and so does Cancer Rising. You are secretive, sensitive, and patriotic.

The Symbol of Cancer is the Crab, which carries its home on its back. When you are threatened, you quickly retreat and hide in your shell.

Cancer is the natural Sign of the Fourth House which relates to the home, family, heritage, foundations, and land. Your emotional stability or instability is the product of your early environment and parental influence.

You are very protective of your family and sensitive to the feelings of others. Of all the signs Cancer Rising is the most emotional and the shyest because of the emotional and receptive nature of your Rising Sign and its ruler.

With Cancer Rising you were born with great sensitivity and you will learn to balance your feelings through relationships that provide you with emotional discipline.

LEO Rising

Quality: Fixed
Element: Fire
Polarity: Masculine
Ruling Planet: The Sun
Symbol: The Lion

Leo Key Declaration: I Create

Those born with Leo Rising are seen as those who know their value. Leo Rising wants to be known for their creativity and their bold leadership.

Leo is a Fixed Fire Sign which gives you the characteristics of stubbornness, determination, and fixity of purpose. As an initiating, active, enthusiastic, passionate, Masculine polarity, you have a flair for drama. You need outlets for your creative expressions and experiences. You have more hope and optimism than any other Sign.

Leo Rising is ruled by our very own Sun, which is a Star, not a Planet. The Sun represents vitality, life, ego, creativity, and expression. Leo can be bigger than life as the Sun wants to shine, create, express, and display.

You are stubborn and never want to admit defeat. You are also rigid in your opinions, are security oriented, and do not like change. You may sacrifice your creativity for your choice of career. As your ability and success rises, so does the likelihood of your becoming egotistical and believing you know better.

The Symbol for Leo is the Royal Lion. You are goal-oriented in actions that will ultimately develop your ego and pride. You are very loving and affectionate and want to be appreciated. A simple praise is a sought-after reward. You want everyone, including yourself, to be rewarded appropriately.

Leo is the natural Sign of the Fifth House which emphasizes children, creativity, and entertainment so it is natural for you to have these characteristics in your life. You see yourself through your creations, which include your children as well as your works of art, and risk-taking feats.

You want to prosper and do well for yourself and your family. You are great at organizing and you make a strong, dynamic leader, who believes you know better than all others. You are inspiring, intuitive, charming, and playful.

With Leo Rising you were born with great passion and you will learn to temper it through the objectivity of those with whom you are in a relationship.

VIRGO Rising

Quality: Mutable
Element: Earth
Polarity: Feminine
Ruling Planet: Mercury
Symbol: The Virgin

Virgo Key Declarations:
I ANALYZE, I SERVE

Those born with Virgo Rising are seen as supportive and needing stability. Virgo Rising wants to be known for their ability to analyze and serve in a practical dedicated way.

Virgo Rising has a natural instinct that will help you in your career, especially in the communication fields. There is a good chance of success if you use your potential constructively.

Virgo is a Mutable Earth Sign which makes you adaptable and grounded. You are a practical multi-tasker. Order is particularly important to you.

Virgo is of the receptive Feminine polarity. You have a practical approach to the material world which helps you discriminate among what is good, better, and best to ultimately bring purity to your life. You seek quality over quantity.

Virgo's ruling Planet is Mercury, the 'Messenger,' the fastest, most detail-oriented Planet motivating you to learn and communicate precisely.

The symbol for Virgo is the Virgin. You are modest and humble. You do not like being put on the spot. You can be overly self-critical. You want to be correct.

Virgo is the natural Sign of the Sixth House which governs matters concerning detail work, health, and service to others. It is natural for you to be interested in the medical field, real estate and occupations that require constant attention to details. You can become overly health conscious. You want perfection in your life. You are kind, meticulous, fastidious, and detailed oriented.

Virgo Rising are the workers of the Zodiac and you are often placed in supporting roles. You enjoy routine responsibilities. You may come across as petty or fussy. You are a critical thinker and need to examine every situation in detail.

With Virgo Rising you were born with material practicality and you will learn spiritual sensitivity from those with which you are in a relationship.

LIBRA Rising

Quality: Cardinal
Element: Air
Polarity: Masculine
Ruling Planet: Venus
Symbol: The Scales

Libra Key Declarations:
I BALANCE, I PARTNER

Those born with Libra Rising are seen as people who love equality in partnerships. Libra Rising wants to be known for their ability to relate to others and exchange ideas in a fair and even way.

The need to relate is a strong element of your personality. You have good manners, have thoughtful remarks, and are a welcomed guest. You are persuasive and will encourage others to see your point of view. You initiate actions toward teamwork, marriage, and business partnerships or close associations.

Libra is a Cardinal Air Sign which gives you leadership and intellectual traits. Libra is of the extroverted Masculine polarity and the ruling Planet is Venus, the 'Lover,' which represents beauty, charm, and sensuality. It motivates you to relate.

The Symbol for Libra is the Scales that seeks balance and justice. Your desire for harmony and balance can lead to indecision. You can easily ignore your personal problems. You are fair and considerate of others and do not want to hurt anyone's feelings.

Libra is the natural Sign of the Seventh House, which is the House of partnerships, justice, and social interaction. You love companionship and enjoy being with one special person.

Because of your strong need for relationships you may rush into commitments too quickly. You need to talk things through with a trusted partner. You can be more concerned with your close relationships than your family ties.

With Libra Rising you were born with a desire to put your own thoughts aside to make peace with others and will learn how to define who 'you' yourself are through your close partnerships.

SCORPIO Rising

Quality: Fixed
Element: Water
Polarity: Feminine
Ruling Planets:
  Mars, Pluto
Symbol: The Scorpion

Scorpio Key Declaration: I DESIRE

Those born with Scorpio Rising can be seen as aggressive and ready to fight battles, but under that exterior is a reserved and cautious person. Scorpio Rising wants to be known for their power and deep personal transformations.

You give a lot of thought, study, and practice to any situation. You desire deep thought, deep study, and deep training. You are goal oriented and work with shared funding or possessions gained through the resources of others.

Scorpio is a Fixed Water Sign which accounts for your Fixed, stubborn nature and intense emotions. Scorpio is a receptive Feminine polarity indicating that you take things into consideration before responding.

Scorpios have two ruling Planets which are the traditional Planet of Mars, the 'Warrior' that fights, and the modern Planet of Pluto, the 'Transformer' that transforms. Scorpio Rising can have intense life experiences that renew and transform. You want to change things. You have a need for power and control and can learn to manipulate in order to maintain it. You need to guard against the extremes of becoming obsessive, possessive, or dictatorial.

The symbol for Scorpio is the Scorpion with a poisonous stinger. With Scorpio Rising you can be suspicious, jealous, unforgiving, and secretive. If you are betrayed, you will get revenge.

Scorpio is the natural Sign of the Eighth House which represents death, passion, sexuality, and taboo issues. Therefore, it is natural for you to be interested in deep spiritual meanings and the afterlife. There is a strong sense of purpose and a need to question every action. You like to solve mysteries, dig things up, and get to the bottom.

You can see your short comings and problems clearly and are always looking to transform yourself into something better. Because of all the self-evaluation you may overlook your own positive qualities.

With Scorpio Rising you were born with a need to control others, but you will learn inner control and self-respect through your committed partnerships.

SAGITTARIUS Rising

Quality: Mutable
Element: Fire
Polarity: Masculine
Ruling Planet: Jupiter
Symbol: The Archer

Sagittarius Key Declarations:
I SEEK, I EXPLORE

Those born with Sagittarius Rising come across as optimistic and pursuing life on a grand scale. Sagittarius Rising wants to be known for taking action in daring physical and spiritual adventures.

You are a truth seeker, eager to explore the world. Sagittarius Rising are the philosophers and spiritual teachers of the Zodiac. You are outgoing, multicultural and love anything international.

Sagittarius is a people-oriented Fire Sign with a Masculine polarity. Both are extroverted and action oriented. A Mutable mode gives you the ability to be adaptable and changeable.

Sagittarius' ruling Planet is Jupiter, the 'Sage,' the largest Planet in the Solar System whose impulse is to explore and expand. Jupiter represents optimism, abundance, and a big appetite for life. Your optimistic outlook leads to great accomplishments. You have a real need for a challenge. You will reach your full potential if you are encouraged.

The symbols for Sagittarius are the Archer as well as the Rainbow. You have strong faith and a positive spirit. You work on developing your mind and can often rise to great spiritual and philosophical heights.

Sagittarius is the natural Sign of the Ninth House that represents truth, integrity, higher education. It is natural for you to seek knowledge. You are the perpetual student always searching for new subjects to explore. You like to be with people on your own intellectual level. You are interested in the world around you and you enjoy higher learning and spirituality.

You need open air and love to be outdoors. You enjoy risky adventures. If you are not challenged, uncharacteristic depression can set in. You have lofty ideas and want your name to be associated with your concepts.

With Sagittarius Rising you were born with the ability to reach for higher truth and you will learn practical reality through your interaction with others.

CAPRICORN Rising

Quality: Cardinal
Element: Earth
Polarity: Feminine
Ruling Planet: Saturn
Symbol: The Goat

Capricorn Key Declaration: I ACHIEVE

Capricorn Rising comes across as being rigid and self-controlled. Capricorn Rising wants to be known for building their career in a practical, honorable way.

You have a sense of reality about yourself and the world. Capricorn is a difficult Rising Sign, with a built-in sense of duty and obligation. Achievement is important to Capricorns. You work hard until you reach your goal.

Capricorn is a Cardinal Sign and is ambitious and enterprising. You are an initiator of action that seeks to enhance your public image, and your business and professional influence.

Capricorn is of the Earth Element that makes you a practical and steady leader. You are of the receptive Feminine polarity that absorbs ideas and thoughts that will help you reach your goals.

Capricorn's ruling Planet is the ringed Planet Saturn, the 'Taskmaster,' representing responsibility. You want an honorable life and your reputation is important to you. You seek status. You have a sense of reality about the world around you but at times have a hard time seeing yourself clearly. You often underestimate yourself and need the compliments of those close to you as reassurance.

The Goat is the symbol for Capricorn. You are able to start from scratch and you are not satisfied until you get to the top of your Mountain. You need the stability of home as your security on your climb to the top.

Capricorn is the natural Sign of the Tenth House which is the House of responsibility, perseverance, ambition, and career. Because of this, it is natural for you to be concerned with the achievement of public recognition resulting in a higher position in the community.

You can display great confidence in some areas of your life and be timid in others. You can feel guilty about almost anything. Your self-confidence waivers and a small set back can lead to depression, which physical exercise can help alleviate.

With Capricorn Rising you were born with the drive to achieve and you will learn about emotional nurturing through your committed partnerships.

AQUARIUS Rising

Quality: Fixed
Element: Air
Polarity: Masculine
Ruling Planets:
Saturn, Uranus
Symbol:
The Waterbearer

Aquarius Key Declaration: I ASPIRE

Those born with Aquarius Rising come across as distant and hard to feel close to, even though they are really friendly, outgoing, and generally upbeat. Aquarius Rising wants to be known for the ability to communicate and institute new ideas for the betterment of humanity.

You are deeply concerned with the betterment of mankind as a whole and have a futuristic understanding about life. You are a humanitarian and are socially aware of the latest trends. You are an innovator and are open to new ideas.

Aquarians are of the Fixed mode indicating you are inflexible and like things to remain the same especially when it comes time for you to change your ways. You are also fixed in your opinions especially when they go against the popular consensus!

You are of the Air Element meaning you are a thinker and can over think any matter. Aquarius is of the positive Masculine polarity suggesting you are outgoing and generally upbeat.

Aquarius' ruling Planets are Saturn, the 'Taskmaster,' the traditional ruler, which motivates your responsibility, and Uranus, the 'Revolutionary,' the modern ruler, which gives you the drive to break with tradition. You are willful, contrary, and happy to be unconventional. You are quite independent so much so that you may sacrifice a permanent relationship for your independence. You feel comfortable with computers and other technical equipment.

The Water Bearer is the symbol for Aquarius. Aquarius is the natural Sign of the Eleventh House, the House of friends, technology, clubs, organizations, and the unique. It is natural for you to relate to large groups of people, but not on a one on one, intimate basis.

You have a deep understanding that is the result of a consistent thought process. You may overthink matters. You are detached, objective and are a good observer of people and life. You like to know what makes other people tick. You also enjoy learning about yourself.

With Aquarius Rising you were born with a philanthropic, public oriented focus and you will learn about your own individuality through your interactions with others.

PISCES Rising

Quality: Mutable
Element: Water
Polarity: Feminine
Ruling Planets:
    Jupiter, Neptune
Symbol: The Fish

Pisces Key Declarations:
I BELIEVE, I DREAM

Those born with Pisces Rising are seen as being compassionate and understanding. Pisces Rising wants to be known as a benevolent, self-sacrificial support to their community.

You are somewhat secretive and do not reveal much of yourself so it is difficult for people to get to know you. You have strong insight into spiritual subjects that can lead you to the study of mystical teachings and the prophetic realms.

Pisces is a Mutable Sign under the flowing Element of Water which is symbolic of flexibility and sensitivity. Your passive Feminine polarity allows you to take in and absorb other people's energies. You connect with others through your sympathetic, supportive, and caring nature. You blend well with others so much so you may disappear into your surroundings. However, you would be sorely missed.

The ruling Planets are Jupiter the 'Sage' as classical ruler which motivates you to explore and expand, and Neptune the 'Dreamer' the modern ruler which seeks out the Divine. You are good at expanding your spirituality. You are idealistic, devoted, and will make sacrifices for others.

The symbol for Pisces is the Fish. You find comfort near the Water. You are sensitive to the people and situations around you.

Pisces is the natural Sign of the Twelfth House of secrets, confinement, institutions, and creativity. For this reason, it is natural for you to experience secret sorrows. You can relate to individuals who may be mentally, emotionally, or physically challenged in some way.

Your work is of real value to your community. You must learn not to under value yourself. You can escape into imagination. Because of self-doubt you can create a different persona and use your imagination to become that character instead of really trying to find yourself.

With Pisces Rising you are born with natural spirituality and you will need the practicality of your partner to ground you.

Your Sun's House
Where Your Sun 'Shines' the Brightest

The Sun represents your life purpose, vitality, and self-expression. Its position in the Natal Chart will reveal the area of life where you are to live out the principles revealed by your Sun which represents the core of your identity.

The House your Sun occupies shows where you apply your power and authority as well as where you display your gifts and talents. This is the area of life in which you take pride. You will be involved in this part of your life and use it intentionally, and it will be used sovereignly by the Lord's leading, to fulfill your purpose.

The House the Sun is in on your Chart will provide insight into the area of your life:

- That will be a natural focus during your life
- Where you express yourself and display your creativity
- Where you achieve and distinguish yourself
- Where you need to stand out and feel special and make your mark
- Where you most want to develop your skills and talents
- Where you always want to improve
- Where your Sun needs to shine

Through participating in the activities associated with this House, you will establish a clearer sense of selfhood, ego, and identity. It can give you clues to a natural vocation or calling. The House your Sun occupies is generally the area of main focus for your life.

The Sun's House can also be an area you struggle in throughout your life. This struggle can be within yourself or with others. They challenge you and ultimately help strengthen and define your life. Sometimes these struggles can be likened to going to battle with the enemies of your soul that are trying to hold you back and obstruct your development in the sphere of experience associated with the Sun's House. Because of this conflict, you feel you can do better than you have already done in this part of your life.

The Cast of Characters

Sun and Moon = The Actors in the Play
(What)

Sign = The Role the Actor is playing
(How)

House = The Stage or Setting the Activity of the Actor
takes place
(Where)

An Orchestrated Play in the Heavens

To further understand the relationship between the Planets, the Signs, and the Houses of the Natal Chart you can envision it as a play.

The Planets, in this case the Sun and the Moon, represent the actors in the play. They each have their parts to perform and symbolize the main actions and drives in the person's makeup. These Planets illustrate the principles that are active. In this case, the Sun illustrates the principles of the Will, and the Moon illustrates the principles of the Emotions.

The Sign in which a Planet is placed indicates the role the actor is playing. It shows the unique character or mode of expression they use to perform the part. The characteristics of the Sign tell us the way the Planet will display, express, and embody the principles the Planet represents.

The House in which a Planet is placed, regardless of Sign, represents the stage or setting where the activity of the Planet takes place. It tells us where we will use and develop the principle of the Planet. It reveals which area of life is involved. There are twelve Houses, or areas of life represented in the Wheel of Life which is the Zodiac. The Sun can be in any of them depending on the time of a person's birth.

The Planet is the 'What,' the Sign is the 'How,' and the House is the 'Where' that the 'What' and 'How' play out in your life.

In order to feel complete and fulfilled you need to be giving expression to your Sun Sign. You naturally strive to develop yourself in the area of life associated with the House your Sun occupies.

To know which specific area of your life the Sun is shining in your Chart, you need to know your Rising Sign, which is the constellation that was on the Eastern horizon at the moment of your birth. The exact time of your birth is needed for this calculation as it sets up the physical position of the areas of your life that are known as Houses in your Natal Chart.

Once you have determined which House your Sun falls in, you can match the activities that are associated with that House with the traits of your Sun and see how these have already played out in your life. It is important to know your birth time as accurately as possible and not just a guess, as the degree on the horizon changes every four minutes.

If you do not know your birth time, continue to study the traits of your Sun Sign. On its own it is a very insightful and important component of the gifts and talents with which you were born. Once you know your birth time, you can explore the following information about the Houses in your Chart.

The Houses

There are 12 Houses and each one covers a unique aspect of life. The House position itself and its meaning always stays the same. However, the Zodiac Sign that occupies the House changes based on the time of birth and is different in each person's Natal Chart.

Listed here are the Names of the Houses, also called 'Gates' in Ancient Astrology, and the areas of life they each represent:

The House	The Area of Life Involved
First House	The House of Life and Individuality
Second House	The House of Resources and Values
Third House	The House of Communication, and Learning
Fourth House	The House of Home and Foundation
Fifth House	The House of Will and Creative Expression
Sixth House	The House of Service and Discipline
Seventh House	The House of Partnerships and Marriage
Eighth House	The House of Death, Transformation, and Other People's Money
Ninth House	The House of Higher Knowledge, and Foreign Places
Tenth House	The House of Responsibility, and Public Status
Eleventh House	The House of Groups, Friends, Hope
Twelfth House	The House of Endings, Seclusion, and Spirituality

These Houses are ordered around the Wheel of Life in their numerical order and their position is always the same. A different Sign of the Zodiac can, and many times will, occupy the House, but the House itself and the area of life it represents always stays the same.

The Zodiac Sign occupying each House adds a unique style to the areas of life that the House represents.

Where You 'Shine' the Best!

With regards to your Sun, the House it is in represents the area in your life where you can best express and radiate the purpose of your Sun.

The House is where the activity of your Sun takes place. When you look to see what House your Sun is in, you are looking at the area in your life where you will need to shine and develop your personality in order to fulfill your life's purpose.

Following are descriptions of the expression of the Sun in each of the twelve Houses.

1st House
The House of Life and Individuality

The First House deals with the personality, the self, appearance, beginnings, personal well-being, the body, first impressions, attitude, identity, inner motivation, and approach to life.

When Your Sun Shines in the First House
The Sun in the First House shines in the area of personality, appearance, and potential for individual power. This is where you express and apply your will, generally by yourself and for yourself. Your personality will be used and developed to fulfill your life's purpose.

The Sun in the First House will dominate the entire Chart since this is the House of Self. It is the only House focused on your own identity. Focusing on 'self' to improve your character traits, as well as to survive, is important. You need to rely on yourself to take care of yourself.

This position carries with it great initiative and powers for leadership. You are creative and have a competitive spirit. You are motivated to be first and to win. You are ambitious and seek success. You need to feel you are a person of importance with a destination. You are not easily swayed by the opinion or desires of others and are determined to choose your own course in life.

Both the First House and the Sun deal with the self so you should be aware of self-centered tendencies and try to counter them whenever possible. With the Sun in the First House you can be the life of the party. With all the effort you put into yourself, you have a lot to offer!

The Sun in the First House is asking you to find all the authentic ways to express your Will through the qualities of the First House. You shine your light through your creative expression and application of your Will through your individuality and personality.

~~~~~~~~~~~~

So God created mankind in his own image,
in the image of God he created them;
male and female he created them.
Genesis 1:27

2nd House
The House of Resources and Values

The Second House deals with resources, livelihood, money, work, earned income, concrete values, self-worth, priorities, moveable possessions, your job, and work ethic.

When Your Sun Shines in the Second House
The Sun in the Second House shines through your resources including earned income, financial resources, movable possessions, self-worth, and work. Your resources will be used and developed to fulfill your life purpose.

The Sun in the Second House gives important clues as to how you will acquire and utilize your resources. It indicates the need to learn the lessons of stewardship and the correct use of material resources as you express your individuality through them. You want the world to know of your success. You may show love to others by giving meaningful gifts.

With your Sun in the Second House, financial and emotional security are important to you. Insecurity may make you possessive of what is yours. Leisurely pleasure is important to you, such as the enjoyment of rich, expensive food in glamorous surroundings.

You will work hard to provide your ever-expanding needs and wants, and your efforts provide material results. You may or may not have a great deal of money or have an easy way to support yourself, but it is essential to use how and where you make your living to develop yourself.

The Sun in the Second House encourages you to shine your light through constructive and beneficial ways to generate and use your resources.

~~~~~~~~~~~~~

To one he gave five bags of gold, to another two bags,
and to another one bag, each according to his ability.
Then he went on his journey. Matthew 25:15

3rd House
The House of Communication and Learning

The Third House deals with the mind, thinking, early education, primary religious instruction, communication, speech, logic, brothers, and sisters, near relatives (not parents), social and community activity, immediate environment, neighborhood interaction, and short distance travel.

When Your Sun Shines in the Third House
The Sun in the Third House shines in intellectual capacity, education, and general spiritual knowledge. Your communication and intellect will be used and developed to fulfill your life purpose.

The need to communicate is vital. You express your individuality through your ideas. You desire to make your mind work and attain knowledge.

With your Sun in the Third House there will be a powerful drive to achieve distinction through intellectual and mental accomplishments. If you did not get a sufficient level of education as a child, you will pursue it at some point in your life.

You are creative with words. Great curiosity makes you eager to investigate new things. Both positive or negative interactions with siblings, especially the oldest, and neighbors will be emphasized.

The Sun in the Third House is encouraging you to shine your light through your ability to express and communicate your ideas and knowledge.

~~~~~~~~~~~~~

May these words of my mouth and this meditation of my heart
be pleasing in your sight, LORD, my Rock and my Redeemer.
Psalm 19:14

4th House
The House of Home and Foundation

The Fourth House deals with home, family, roots, parent, ancestors, heritage, early family foundation, self-care, domestic life, land, comfort, and security.

When Your Sun Shines in the Fourth House
The Sun in the Fourth House shines on the roots and ancestry of your family. A foundation based on home, family, and traditions will be used and developed to fulfill your purpose.

Home and family are especially important to you. Your parents are a strong influence in your life, either positively or negatively.

With your Sun in the Fourth House, the first part of your life may be a struggle followed by increasing prosperity and security later on in your life. Understanding the background of your relationship with parents, as well as your heritage, is essential for providing a foundation for your life. You are overly concerned with the past and need to develop an attitude that looks to the future.

There is a need for safety and a strong interest in land, houses, and natural resources. You express your individuality in your home. The security of your home is important to you. You are creative with your home and family. You may work with your family or work at home.

135

The Sun in the Fourth House encourages you to shine your light through establishing a secure home, foundation, and family.

~~~~~~~~~~~~~

For no one can lay any foundation other than the one already laid, which is Jesus Christ. 1 Corinthians 3:11

5th House
The House of Will and
Creative Expression

The Fifth House emphasizes your Will, self-expression, fertility, children, joy, pleasure, romance, speculation, drama, a childlike spirit, games of chance, speculation, all places of enjoyment, entertainment, schools, sporting events, and creative talents and hobbies.

When Your Sun Shines in the Fifth House
The Sun shines brightly in the Fifth House as it is the natural House of the Sun and the Sign of Leo, which is associated with ego and creative expression. The expression of your Will, your being, your creativity will be used and developed to fulfill the purpose of your life.

The Fifth House is the House of children, so your children will be at the forefront of your life, either positively or negatively. Parents need to be careful not to live their lives vicariously through their children.

Your need for positive acknowledgement through love and your sexual interest can be high. You can be overly dramatic. You express your individuality in romantic and fun settings. You will

137

spend a good amount of time seeking pleasure. You have a Sunny disposition and at times seem to be overly optimistic and naïve.

You are highly competitive and seek achievement in sports, music, theater, or other artistic pursuits. There is a great need to be reassured, noticed, appreciated, and admired. You can be the life of the party.

The Sun in the Fifth House encourages you to shine your light through your love of life and a powerful desire toward creative self-expression.

~~~~~~~~~~~~~

We have different gifts, according to the grace given
to each of us. If your gift is prophesying, then prophesy in
accordance with your faith; if it is serving, then serve;
if it is teaching, then teach; if it is to encourage, then give
encouragement; if it is giving, then give generously;
if it is to lead, do it diligently; if it is to show mercy,
do it cheerfully. Romans 12:6-8

6th House
The House of Service and Discipline

The Sixth House deals with disciplines such as health, fitness, diet, work habits, analysis, systems, organization, hobbies, small pets, sickness, injuries, sense of usefulness, and service given to others.

When Your Sun Shines in the Sixth House
The Sun in the Sixth House shines on the focus of your health, well-being, and your work habits. Your service to others and taking care of your health will be used and developed to fulfill the purpose of your life.

With the Sun in the Sixth House, there may be a great concentration on ailments and concern about diets and health. You instinctively know how to take care of your health.

You take pride in your work and your service. You are likely to be highly proficient and creative at what you do and how you do it but at times it may be hard for your light to be seen. There is a sense of duty and routine, but if you do not receive outward appreciation for your work it may lead to you being stuck in a rut or rebelling against your employer.

Expressing your individuality at work and being of service to others in a positive way will bring satisfaction.

The Sun in the Sixth House encourages you to shine your light through your work and service to others.

~~~~~~~~~~~~~

Each of you should use whatever gift you have received to serve others, as faithful stewards of God's grace in its various forms.
1 Peter 4:10

Whatever you do, work heartily, as for the Lord and not for men... Colossians 3:23 ESV

7th House
The House of Partnerships
and Marriage

The Seventh House deals with committed relationships, partnerships, business relationships, legal contracts, equality, open enemies, and interpersonal style.

When Your Sun Shines in the Seventh House
The Sun in the Seventh House shines through close, personal, and one on one relationships with other people. Partnership and close relationship will be used and developed to fulfill your life purpose.

Being with others is your main path toward the full realization of your potential no matter how independent you try to be. Total commitment and attention to a partner can be of prime importance.

With your Sun in the Seventh House, you are creative in partnerships and can attract strong, loyal, and capable close friends. This position supports popularity and self-confidence. You can be good at public relations, sales, and promotions.

Marriage is important to you. You express your individuality with your partner. Keeping the balance between self and your partner will be essential as the Sun in the Seventh House can either lose their identity in that of their partner's or become disrespectful of the individual expression of others.

The Sun in the Seventh House encourages you to shine your light through your close personal relationship with others.

~~~~~~~~~~~~~

Dear friends, let us love one another,
for love comes from God.
Everyone who loves has been born of God
and knows God.
1 John 4:7

8th House
The House of Death, Transformation and Other People's Money

The Eighth House deals with deep life changing experiences, death, inheritance, regeneration, secrets, deep spiritual insights, intuition, intimacy, shared finances, taxes, loans, investments, assets, taboo issues, other people's money, and partners' resources.

When Your Sun Shines in the Eighth House

The Sun in the Eighth House shines, though a bit darkly at times, through the purposeful force and the great emotional intensity of this House. The deeper mysteries of life such as death, rebirth, and survival are of interest and will be used and developed to fulfill your life's purpose, especially in your later years. It will be as you grow and change throughout your life.

Transformation is a major association with the Eighth House. You may have experienced substantial losses in your life and survived many events that brought you to the edge of what you thought you could bear. These severe events transformed your life and your survival made it necessary to grow in your self-knowledge, self-improvement, and inner strength causing you to grow, develop and eventually change. Through this knowledge you can empower others to develop their talents and resources.

You may be involved with other people's money and resources. You express your individuality through your ability to probe deeply into life's mysteries. There is a need to experience a deep level of spiritual reality that can lead to the awareness and knowledge of the reality of the One True God.

The Sun in the Eight House empowers you to shine your light through deep personal transformations and self-improvement.

~~~~~~~~~~~~~

Oh, the depth of the riches of the wisdom and knowledge of God!
How unsearchable his judgments, and his paths
beyond tracing out! Romans 11:33

9th House
The House of Higher Knowledge and Foreign Places

The Ninth House deals with wisdom, philosophy, spirituality, higher education, the legal system, law, religion, mystical matters, ideals, sleep, dreams, publishing and foreign places, cross-cultural relations, and long-distance travel.

When Your Sun Shines in the Ninth House
The Sun in the Ninth House shines through what is far away, whether it be far away through physical travel, mental travel, or spiritual travel. The Ninth House is traditionally the House of God. There is an interest in spiritual and religious pursuits and the will to search the realms of higher education, law, and philosophy for truth and higher knowledge. These will be used and developed to fulfill your life's purpose.

Intellectual growth for body, mind, and spirit are the emphasis of the Ninth House. You are creative in exploring various philosophies. You express your individuality through your beliefs. You desire to be an authority in some aspect of higher knowledge. You have strong moral convictions which may become narrow-minded and bigoted.

You are genuinely interested in the larger view of life and the laws and traditions governing it. Learning how to make your beliefs practical will empower you to develop your potential and make the most of the driving force of your Sun.

The Sun in the Ninth House encourages you to shine your light through dynamic interest in philosophy and spiritual beliefs.

~~~~~~~~~~~~~

Set your minds on things above, not on earthly things.
Colossians 3:2

10th House
The House of Responsibility
and Public Status

The Tenth House deals with career, social standing, status, authority, reputation, power, public roles, advancement, ambition, boss, long-term goals, aspirations, structure, public image, men, experts, and recognition.

When Your Sun Shines in the Tenth House
The Sun in the Tenth House shines by making its mark on the world. This is one of the strongest Houses in the Chart, second only to the First. You must establish yourself out in the world. Your profession and public persona will be used as a vehicle to develop and fulfill your purpose.

Worldly progress is of most importance to you and is a driving force in your life. Increased prestige and status bring additional responsibility. Many politicians and public figures have their Sun in the Tenth House. You are creative in your career. You conduct yourself in a dignified and distinguished manner.

With your Sun in the Tenth House, you work hard to develop the necessary knowledge and skills to receive honor and recognition. You want to be a good example for others and moral responsibility is important to you.

You express your individuality from a position of power and have a strong will to succeed. You must shine your light in places and situations where it will be seen. You may not feel comfortable in the spotlight, but you will regret not living up to your potential.

The Sun in the Tenth House encourages you to shine your light through your ambition to attain positions of power, responsibility, and authority.

~~~~~~~~~~~~~

"In the same way, let your light shine before others, that they may see your good deeds and glorify your Father in heaven."
Matthew 5:14-16

11th House
The House of Groups, Friends, Hopes

The Eleventh House deals with friends, community, future, humanitarianism, social awareness, hopes, wishes, dreams, gifts, technology, allies, social groups, ideals, philanthropy, altruism, the unexpected, unique, different, friends, stepchildren, social life, clubs, and organizations.

When Your Sun Shines in the Eleventh House
The Sun in the Eleventh House shines through involvement in group activities, especially those with a humanitarian foundation. Your group associations and friendships will be used and developed to fulfill your purpose.

The Sun in the Eleventh House is associated with prosperity that comes from connecting with others. This tells you there are beneficial connections for you to make and that you will be helped by friends with powerful influence. You can have many friends and be held in a high esteem.

With your Sun in the Eleventh House, you are creative in groups and can be a great source of inspiration to others. You have ambition to work with groups whose members share the same hopes and dreams. You express your individuality through group activities.

149

You have a concern for all humanity and the suffering of the world. You have a sense of brotherhood, but close relationships are rare. You distance yourself from others to maintain independence as you focus on the whole of humanity, not the individual. The more you put yourself in the company of like-minded people the faster you will travel on your route of your life's purpose.

The Sun in the Eleventh House encourages you to shine your light through involvement with your friends, associates, and groups.

~~~~~~~~~~~~~

*How good and pleasant it is when God's people
live together in unity! Psalm 133:1*

12th House
The House of Endings, Seclusion, Spirituality

The Twelfth House deals with psychological strengths and weaknesses, spirituality, healing, endings, closure, old age, what's hidden, subconscious, sacrificial service, faith, limiting beliefs, behind the scenes, private life, institutions, hospitals, prisons, secrets, secret enemies, and self-undoing.

When Your Sun Shines in the Twelfth House

The Sun in the Twelfth House shines when you are alone, in a peaceful and quiet place. Your will is directed toward exploring the depths of your mind and fantasy. Your spiritual sensitivity and self-sacrifice will be used and developed to fulfill your purpose.

This is the most withdrawn of all Houses and you need to spend some time each day alone to recharge. The people whose Sun falls in this House quietly show their creativity behind the scenes. You can be excessively shy, which can cause you to be lonely and estranged from normal contacts.

Psychology and spiritual growth interest you and you give serious thought to important life issues. An understanding of God and His comfort is developed and grown in the Twelfth House.

You have special healing energy that becomes available only after you have been healed of your own deepest wounds. Through the sorrows of life, you learn, study, and understand how pain and suffering work, and you realize that your character has been strengthened. You want to help those who are struggling or have been bound in sorrows themselves.

You express your individuality through service in large institutions such as hospitals, asylums, or places of spiritual or physical retreat. You often hide your talents and need someone else to promote them for you. You may unconsciously be your own worst enemy through self-sabotage.

The Sun in the Twelfth House encourages you to shine your light in the background through service and sacrifice to others.

~~~~~~~~~~~~~~

Carry each other's burdens, and in this way
you will fulfill the law of Christ. Galatians 6:2

And without faith it is impossible to please God,
because anyone who comes to him must believe that he exists
and that he rewards those who earnestly seek him.
Hebrews 11:16

Digging Deeper
Understanding Yourself and Others

In order to understand yourself and others better, it is helpful to know these additional characteristics of the Zodiac Signs.

The Elements of Matter

The 12 Zodiac signs are organized into four groups. Each group of Signs shares similar characteristics that can help you to further understand the underlying structure of the Zodiac. These four groups are based on the Elements that were present when God created the Earth.

These Elements are known as the Triplicities in Astrology, as there are three signs in each of the four Elements. These Elements are the first and most revealing of the traits of each Sign and are based on the components of Creation.

Elements in Scripture

The Elements are listed by God in the 1st chapter of Genesis (Parenthesis added by Author):

> Now the earth (1) was formless and empty, darkness was over the surface of the deep, and the Spirit (2) of God was hovering over the waters (3). And God said, "Let there be light (4)," and there was light. (Genesis 1:2-3)

This verse shows the four Elements of 1) Earth, 2) Air, 3) Water, and 4) Fire.

Elements of Fire, Earth, Air and Water

According to Ancient tradition, everything on our Earth is made from differing amounts of the Elements of Fire, Earth, Air, and Water.

These four Elements can be understood in four different ways: physically, psychologically, spiritually, and esoterically. The physical properties of the Elements are all based on atoms and how they are spaced in relation to one another. These make up the four states of matter. They are plasma/Fire, solid/Earth, gas/Air, and liquid/Water. They operate within the laws of nature that God put into place.

They can be described as follows:

Fire – is the spark of life that never dies. Fire has electrical and creative energy. Fire rises up but must be connected to the Earth to exist.

Water – has magnetic properties; it nurtures and sustains. Water as liquid spreads out unless it is contained. It tends to overflow its vessel but when too contained it can become a significant force. Water always finds its way back to the sea.

Air – is invisible. Air is a detaching Element and allows the two main Elements, Fire, and Water, to co-exist. It is calm, ethereal, and easily disturbed. It is of little weight, but it is unquestionably there.

Earth – binds Fire, Water, and Air in various amounts, and makes it possible to form together materials with different properties. The Earth is strong and rigid. It takes a lot of Fire, Air, and Water to shape the Earth.

The Elements of Fire, Earth, Air and Water each represent an essential type of energy that interacts with and complements the other Elements in our physical lives. The Elements that form the physical world are also included in man's character.

The scientific properties of the Elements can also be used in a psychological and spiritual sense.   By understanding the characteristics and nature of the four Elements we can adapt their essence and use them metaphorically to understand our human nature. They   describe the unique personality types that are associated with each astrological Sign.

Element Fire – passion, action
Element Earth – material, stability
Element Air – intellect, communication
Element Water – emotions, intuition

These Elements are repeated in this order three times in the Zodiac, and so we have a Biblical order.

The Constellations and
The Triplicities
– Fire, Earth, Air, Water -

Aries – Fire	**Leo – Fire**	**Sagittarius – Fire**
Taurus – Earth	**Virgo – Earth**	**Capricorn – Earth**
Gemini – Air	**Libra – Air**	**Aquarius – Air**
Cancer – Water	**Scorpio – Water**	**Pisces – Water**

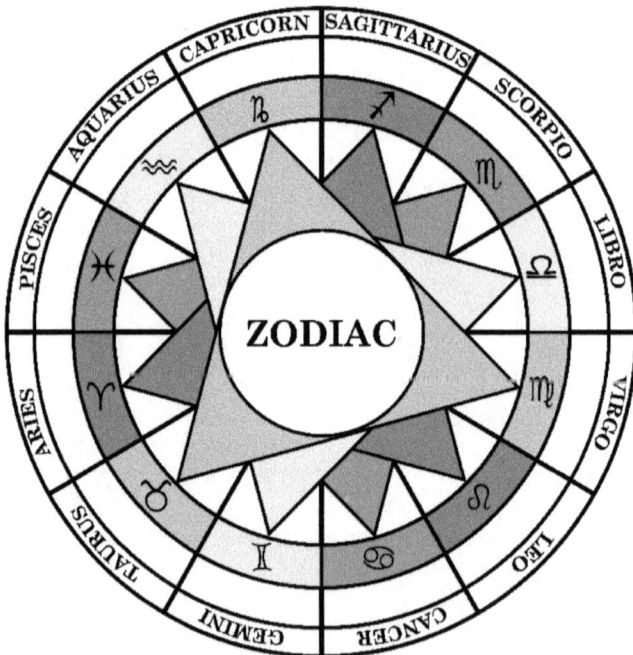

© can stock photo / hibrida13

Elemental Groupings,
How we experience and process the world around us

Each Zodiac Sign is associated with one of the four Elements and are designated as either a Fire Sign, Earth Sign, Air Sign, or Water Sign. The four Elements work according to the laws of nature and reflect the basic character traits, emotions, behavior, and thinking of the individual through the Signs of the Zodiac.

Three of the twelve Signs each share the same Element and have that Element in common in their makeup. The Elements give us an underlying common basis for understanding each Sign.

>   **FIRE** – Aries, Leo, Sagittarius
>   – each have passion and action in common
>   **EARTH** – Taurus, Virgo, Capricorn
>   – each have materiality and stability in common
>   **AIR** – Gemini, Libra, Aquarius
>   – each have intellect and communication in common
>   **WATER** – Cancer, Scorpio, Pisces
>   – each have emotions and intuition in common

The difference between the three Signs within a triplicity is the degree, proportion, or strength of the Element that is expressed. Each Sign has varying degrees of the Element, but the foundational characteristic of the Element is the same. Astrology helps us identify these elemental energies as reflected in our Natal Charts so we can acquire a better understanding of our positive and negative traits.

The Four Temperaments

The traits of the four Elements can also be used to describe the four types of Temperaments in Man. In the body the four Elements of Fire, Earth, Air, and Water are known as the four Humors and they are the basis for the four Temperaments of Choleric, Melancholic, Sanguine, and Phlegmatic, respectively. These temperaments have been explored in many self-discovery books and are well accepted. They were originally used by Ancient doctors like Hippocrates, to classify people and health conditions.

A mixture of these Elements/Temperaments is found in each person. The Sun, the Moon, and the Rising Sign shown in a person's Natal Chart are each in a Sign, and that Sign is associated with an Element. When we combine the Elements with the Temperaments, we can see a fundamental picture of the underlying structure of personality.

Element	Temperament	Characteristics	Zodiac Signs
Fire	Choleric	Passion, action, enthusiasm	Aries, Leo, Sagittarius
Earth	Melancholic	Material, money, practical	Taurus, Virgo, Capricorn
Air	Sanguine	Thought, communication, intellectual	Gemini, Libra, Aquarius
Water	Phlegmatic	Emotions, love, intuitive	Cancer, Scorpio, Pisces

In general terms, science, and tradition state that Fire/Choleric Signs are by nature enthusiastic, Earth/Melancholic Signs are practical, Air/Sanguine Signs are intellectual and have a need to communicate, and Water/Phlegmatic Signs are emotional.

Whichever Element or Temperament is most dominant in a person's Chart will determine if they have an overall Choleric,

Melancholic, Sanguine or Phlegmatic nature. When we identify and give a name to our Temperament, we will better understand our qualities. When we know someone else's temperament, we will also better understand their qualities.

How these Elements display themselves are according to the function of the Planet expressing them. The function of the Sun, the Moon and the Rising Sign will each display the characteristics of the Element with which they are associated in their own unique way: The Sun shines – sets the goal; The Moon reflects – makes it real; The Rising Sign projects – the method used to accomplish it.

Following are some examples of the identifiable ways that the Element would undergird and set the tone for the expression of each of the Luminaries.

If the **Sun** shines through a Fire Sign,
the individual will be enthusiastic.

If the **Sun** shines through an Earth Sign,
the individual will be practical.

If the **Sun** shines through an Air Sign,
the individual will be intellectual.

If the **Sun** shines through a Water Sign,
the individual will be emotional.

If the **Moon** reflects through a Fire Sign,
the emotions will be enthusiastic.

If the **Moon** reflect through an Earth Sign,
the emotions will be practical.

If the **Moon** reflects through an Air Sign,
the emotions will be intellectual.

If the **Moon** reflects through a Water Sign,
the emotions will be intuitive.

If the **Rising Sign** projects through a Fire Sign,
the persona will be enthusiastic.

If the **Rising Sign** projects through an Earth Sign,
the persona will be practical.

If the **Rising Sign** projects through an Air Sign,
the persona will be intellectual.

If the **Rising Sign** projects through a Water Sign,
the persona will be emotional.

This is one reason why people tend to display different
Temperaments when they are in different settings, environments,
or situations in their lives.

As an example, a person can be aggressive and outgoing in public
and passive and quiet at home. Their Sun may be in the 10th House
and in an outgoing Fire/Choleric Sign and their Moon may be the
5th House in a passive Water/Phlegmatic Sign.

This, along with other aspects in the Chart, accounts for any
seemingly contradictory display of personality in different areas
of life as expressed in the Houses.

Elemental Compatibilities

How do these Elements interact with one another? How do they
display themselves in our personality? How can we understand
them in our interactions with one another? Let us use
compatibility as an example.

In science there are laws of nature that govern the way Elements
interact. As we have seen, each of the four Elements is associated
with its own temperament. Each Element has two qualities. The
qualities of each Element are the key to understanding scientific
compatibility. There are certain scientific reactions that can be
related to our human reactions as our Elements react to the
Elements of another individual.

Fire – Passionate, active, courageous, energetic
- Consists of Hot and Dry -

Air – Intellectual, sensible, logical, clear-sighted
- Consists of Hot and Wet -

Water – Emotional, intuitive, sensitive
- Consists of Cold and Wet -

Earth – Practical, down to Earth, materialistic
- Consists of Cold and Dry -

If we think about how these would interact within nature, we can relate to how they might interact in our lives. This is easy on paper, but not so easy in real life, with real people and real-life situations, but it is a starting point which will lead to changes in our behavior, and with our understanding of others.

Knowing the Elemental compatibilities helps clarify our own personalities. We can look at the Elements of our own Sun, Moon and Rising Signs and see how each of their Elements relate.

If we have an Earth Sun (will) with a Water Rising (mind), but an Air Moon (emotion), we can see that Air Moon may be inhibited in expressing emotions due to the conflict of the Elements of the Water Rising and the Earth Sun.

This will help us to understand why we may be having trouble understanding our own feelings which may cause internal conflict and misunderstanding of others. Recognizing the issue is the first step in making adjustments.

This is helpful to know when trying to communicate with others who have Elements that are opposite to our own. A Fire Sign may have an excited, passionate, risky idea and a Water Sign may put the Fire out by being too security conscious to try such a wild idea!

On the other hand, if a Fire Sign communicates with an Air Sign, the Air can fuel the Fire and the ideas can be fanned into flames! All the Elements work together in some way and some are naturally harmonious. Some combinations are harder than others to work through. Depending on the determination and the need, they can work out any differences. They also need to be considered within the context of life in which they are operating.

We must remember that we are not locked into the Temperament of any dominant Element. Everyone is born with free will. We have the ability to use the principles of the Elements to identify qualities that are part of our makeup and those we want to develop in our character. We can also work to transform and improve our negative traits in order to live in peace and fulfill our God given purpose.

Each Element has the ability to do something the others cannot. The Triplicities indicate the abilities present in the Zodiac Signs based on their Element of Fire, Earth, Air or Water. They are available for our use.

The Sun Sign's Element is not the only factor used in determining compatibility. We also look at the Elements associated with the Moon Sign, the Rising Sign, and the other Planets. The Sun is an excellent place to start to check compatibility with someone else because it is a major factor in everyone's Natal Chart and most people know their Sun Sign.

Understanding the characteristics of the Elements and Temperaments can help us to better understand each other and to provide insight into working together more harmoniously. And if not harmoniously, then we can agree to disagree harmoniously!

The nature of our personalities can be seen in the following descriptions of the Elements. They also indicate qualities that are available for us to use and develop in our lifetime.

Fire, Earth, Air, Water Descriptions

MASCULINE
CHOLERIC
The Fire Signs are:
Aries, Leo, Sagittarius

FIRE

The nature of Fire Signs is to make things happen by creating a 'spark.' They tend to be passionate, optimistic, dynamic, and temperamental. They get angry quickly, but they also forgive easily. They are daring adventurers with energy and vigor. They are physically strong, courageous, and are a source of inspiration to others. Fire signs are intelligent, self-aware, creative and can be aggressive. They are faithful and idealistic people always ready for action. Fire signs use their intuition to make decisions.

Fire Signs seek to display leadership in the following ways:

Aries – to lead by initiating and directing new endeavors
Leo – to manage by stabilizing and strengthening groups
Sagittarius – to motivate by inspiring in spiritual, legal, and religious arenas

Too Much Fire: Can be argumentative, irritable, jealous, greedy, vindictive, and can display hate or anger and may become violent or destructive

Lack of Fire: Lack of vision, lack of imagination, lack of energy

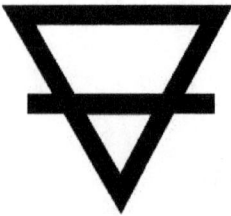

EARTH

FEMININE
MELANCHOLIC
The Earth Signs are:
Taurus, Virgo, Capricorn

The nature of Earth Signs is to be practical and stable. Earth signs are grounded in consistency, responsibility, reliability, and ambition. They are the ones that bring us down to Earth. A strong Earth will bring ideas into reality and give them form. They are mostly conservative and realistic, but they can also be very emotional and depressing. They are connected to our material reality and can be focused on material goods. They are practical, stable, punctual, respectful, careful, and loyal. They stick by those close to them through hard times and can be a stable base. Earth is known to be realistic and useful. Earth signs use their five senses of touch, taste, smell, see and hear to make decisions.

Earth Signs seek to build in a practical, steadfast way in the following ways:

Taurus – to accumulate and manage money and other resources
Virgo – to construct material objects essential to man, especially maintaining the body
Capricorn – to build and manage business and governmental enterprises

Too Much Earth: Stuffiness, laziness, timidity, too predictable, immovable
Lack of Earth: Not well grounded, too lighthearted of an approach to life

MASCULINE SANGUINE

The Air Signs are:

Gemini, Libra, Aquarius

AIR

The nature of Air Signs concerns the mental and intellectual aspect of man. They are rational, social, and love communication and relationships with other people. They are thinkers, communicators, analytical, intellectual, and friendly. They have a trusting nature. They are thoughtful, positive, and optimistic. They love good books, philosophical discussions, and social gatherings. They can deal with abstracts and can be superficial. They enjoy giving advice, but do not receive it well. They use the function of their minds to process information, knowledge, ideas, and concepts to make decisions.

Air Signs seek to communicate and exchange ideas in the following ways:

Gemini – to acquire, use and communicate factual information
Libra – to weigh and balance information, making fair comparisons
Aquarius – to understand universal principles to help the well-being of humanity

Too much Air: Lack of perseverance, can be dishonest, gossip, cunning, backbiting, verbosity, fickleness, touchiness, grumpiness
Lack of Air: Inability to think things through to come to a conclusion

FEMININE
PHLEGMATIC
The Water Signs are:
Cancer, Scorpio, Pisces

WATER

The nature of Water Signs deals with the realm of emotion and feeling. They operate with sensitivity, deep spirituality, and intense emotions. They are highly intuitive and aware of the atmosphere. They are mysterious and rarely do anything openly. Strong Water souls are understanding and compassionate. They internalize other people's feelings. Water signs enjoy reflective conversations and intimacy. They are introverted, introspective, and gentle. They are available to emotionally support their loved ones. Water signs use their feelings to accept or reject things depending on their likes and dislikes to make decisions.

Water Signs seek to create and sustain emotional bonds in the following ways:

Cancer – to create strong emotional bonds with home and family
Scorpio – to uncover the deep secrets and mysteries of life
Pisces – to develop strong spiritual sensitivity, intimate feeling toward the Infinite

Too much Water: Indifference, heartlessness, laziness, indolence, rigidity, lack of daring, lack of concern, unstableness, dejection
Lack of Water: Inability to understand emotions, inability to understand what upsets them and others

166

Modes,
The Way You Operate

Each Sign operates in a Mode that is either Cardinal, Fixed or Mutable. The Modes show the rate and manner that the Elemental energy of the Sign is moving. They are based on where the Zodiac Sign falls within each season. Astrologically the Modes, also called quadruplicities, indicate the Signs' Mode of operation based on the Signs' position within the seasons of the year, either Spring, Summer, Fall, or Winter.

The cycles of the seasons are natural occurrences. Each season has a Month at the beginning, middle and end. The beginning Month is called Cardinal. The middle Month is called Fixed. The last Month is called Mutable. These Modes are based on their transitional ability within that season. Every mode has four Signs associated with it.

Cardinal Constellations begin the seasons of Spring, Summer, Fall and Winter.

The first Month of the Zodiac Year is Aries which is the first Month of Spring and begins around March 21st each year.

The first Month of the Spiritual calendar is Nissan. The Bible states that the Month in which Passover falls shall be the first Month of the year:

> The LORD said to Moses and Aaron in Egypt,
> "This Month is to be for you the first Month,
> the first Month of your year." Exodus 12:1-2

This first Month is Nissan on the Hebrew Calendar, known as God's Calendar. God's Calendar is a Lunar Calendar and is different than the Julian or Gregorian calendars that we typically use which start the year on January 1st.

Nissan (Aviv in early Hebrew) is the beginning of the Spiritual year as well as the Zodiacal year and it is the Lunar Month which begins the Spring season. Nissan is the Zodiac Sign of Aries in English and it is a Cardinal Constellation. As we follow through the year the four Signs that mark the beginning of the four seasons are the Cardinal Signs of Aries, Cancer, Libra, and Capricorn.

Cardinal Signs "lead" the seasons of the year, so this Mode indicates initiation, beginnings, and strong movement. Using the Zodiacal and Lunar Calendar, the Cardinal Signs that lead the seasons are Aries, the beginning of Spring at the Spring Equinox (March 21st); Cancer, the beginning of Summer at the Summer Solstice (June 21st); Libra, the beginning of Autumn at the Autumn Equinox (September 21st); and Capricorn, the beginning of Winter at the Winter Solstice (December 21st).

Cardinal signs have the ability to act directly and decisively in current situations. They can start and develop new ideas in the area of life, or the House, they are involved with. A person with their Sun in a Cardinal Sign is most likely a leader in the area of life indicated by the House it occupies.

Fixed Signs are "Fixed" solidly in the middle of each season. In the Tropical Zodiac, the Signs that are Fixed in the middle of the season are Taurus, the middle of Spring; Leo, the middle of Summer; Scorpio, the middle of Autumn; and Aquarius, the middle of Winter.

Fixed signs achieve results over long periods of time through persistence, determination, and unwavering perseverance. Goal oriented, reliable, and concerned with the future, they are the builders of the Zodiac. They are not easily swayed once their mind is made up. They can be stubborn and rigid. It is hard for them to change and prefer things to remain the same. In order to feel secure, the person with their Sun in a Fixed Sign wants their home, work, income, or social status to be 'Fixed' and stable.

Interestingly, the Fixed Signs are associated with the faces of the Living Creatures, or Cherubim, described as being around the throne of God in Ezekiel (1:10, 10:14) and Revelation (4:7).

And the first creature was like a lion,
and the second creature like a calf,
and the third creature had a face as of a man,
and the fourth creature was like a flying eagle.
Revelation 4:7 ASV

The Lion represents the Fixed Sign Leo. The Calf, or Ox or Bull, represents the Fixed Sign of Taurus. The face of a man represents the Fixed Sign of Aquarius. The flying eagle represents Scorpio. Along with other meanings, these Fixed Signs represent the 'Fixed' stability of God in the Heavens and in our lives.

Every good and perfect gift is from above,
coming down from the Father of the heavenly lights,
who does not change like shifting shadows. James 1:17

Mutable Signs "transition" out of each season. Mutable months provide the transition periods from one season to the next. The four Mutable constellations at this time in history are Gemini, the end of Spring; Virgo, the end of Summer; Sagittarius, the end of Autumn; and Pisces, the end of Winter. Mutable signs indicate adaptability, variety, and changeability in dealing with circumstances of all kinds. They are flexible and resourceful in emergencies. Mutable signs deal with transitions as they travel from one season. The person with their Sun in a Mutable Sign can be traveling, communicating, and adapting regularly as features of their lives, as the Mutable signs move, communicate, and adapt between the seasons.

Season	Cardinal	Fixed	Mutable
Spring	Aries	Taurus	Gemini
Summer	Cancer	Leo	Virgo
Autumn	Libra	Scorpio	Sagittarius
Winter	Capricorn	Aquarius	Pisces

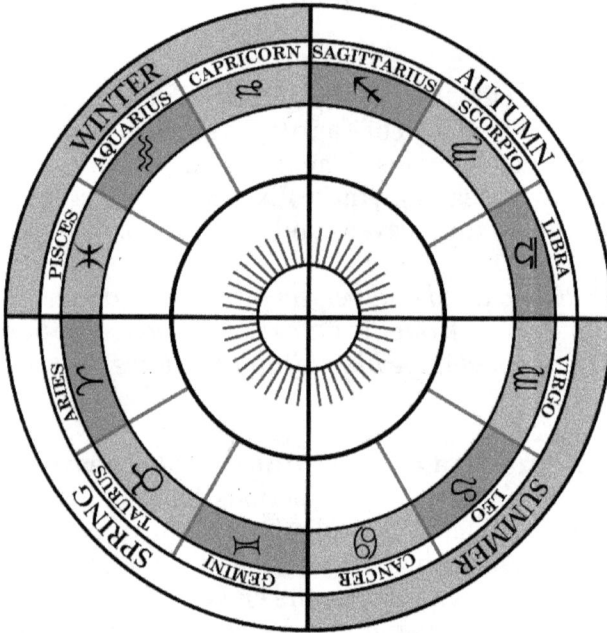

© Can Stock Photo, Inc. / Hibrida 13

How each Mode handles a problem:

As a general example of the different ways in which the Modes express themselves in a personality, we can look at their behavior in handling a difficult problem. The Cardinal Signs will try to figure out a new way to solve the problem quickly, and if it does not work fast enough, they quit and move on. The Fixed Signs will work on the problem until it is solved, and they will not give up regardless of how hard it is or how long it takes. The Mutable Signs adapt or just move on out of the situation!

Sign Polarities

There are two polarities in Astrology. Polarity is illustrated in the balance of a magnet with a positive charge at one end and a negative charge at the other.

The polarities are referred to as Masculine and Feminine, positive and negative, or active and passive. Each of the Elements is either Masculine or Feminine. This does not represent gender as in male or female, instead it applies to their energy and whether they are generally initiating or receptive in nature. Polarities give us the ability to balance areas of our lives. We are often attracted to those who balance our polarity.

Each polarity has six Signs associated with it. They are arranged in alternating order one Sign to the next through all the twelve Signs.

The Fire and Air Signs are Masculine, positive, and aggressive. They are the odd-numbered signs of the Zodiac which are Aries, Gemini, Leo, Libra, Sagittarius, and Aquarius. Masculine is active energy that tends to be self-initiating and takes action to achieve results. They act rather than waiting for results to come to them. They project energies out into the world.

The Water and Earth Signs are Feminine, negative, and receptive. They are the even numbered signs of the Zodiac which are Taurus, Cancer, Virgo, Scorpio, Capricorn, and Pisces. Feminine is passive energy. They can act forcibly if needed but they usually wait for things to come to them and then they will respond. They are passive and interact with whatever happens to come their way. They absorb and accept situations and things.

In the context of polarity, the Sun represents the positive polarity, aggressive or Masculine principle, and therefore, the father or other male authority figures in our lives. The Moon represents the negative polarity, receptive or Feminine principle, and therefore, the mother or other female nurturing figures in our lives.

In your Natal Chart, your Sun, Moon and Rising Signs are each in either a positive/Masculine or a negative/Feminine Sign.

Positive and negative are always in balance in nature. Your personality may be more positive in one area and more negative in another one. You will be attracted to other people who fill your polarity void. This is especially the case in committed relationships and partnerships, and the basis of 'opposites attract.'

There is a natural flow of energy and we are constantly drawn towards other people (almost magnetically) who complement the energy in our Natal Charts. These opposites can cause conflicts when the energies get out of balance. Working out the conflicts balances the energies.

Polarity gives us the ability to learn to balance areas of our lives that are either too much of one or the other. It is a means of bringing balance into our lives.

Ruling Planet
The Ruling Planet of your Chart

The Sun, the Moon and the Rising Sign are the most prominent markers in your Natal Chart. These make up your Primary Star Pattern and are the specific Luminaries we are focusing on in this book.

Where these markers are located on your Natal Chart will give you the fundamentals of understanding yourself and your purpose. Everything else in your Chart will either be supporting or challenging the work of the Luminaries.

In addition to the Luminaries there are eight Planets in our Solar System that God created to work together with the Luminaries. They add a deeper dimension to interpreting your Natal Chart. These eight Planets in order starting from the closest to the Sun are Mercury, Venus, Mars, Jupiter, Saturn, Uranus, Neptune, and Pluto.

The Planet that is associated with your Rising Sign is called the Chart Ruler and it gives additional information about your inner motivation and ability to relate to the world.

While the Rising Sign describes your persona (the personality you show to the world), the Ruling Planet shows the energy behind that persona. It shows the type of initiating impulse behind the way you receive, process, and then project the energy of the world. The Planet that rules your Rising Sign will give insight into the direction of your life and the area of life that will be prominent in fulfilling your life's purpose.

The Planets in our Solar System shown with their identifying glyph in their order from the Sun.

© Can Stock Photos / sermax55

Listed below are the Sun, the Moon, the five traditional and three modern Planets along with their Hebrew names, The Signs they are associated with as well as their primary impulse.

Ruling Planet	Hebrew Name	Signs	Traditional Role	Primary Impulse
Sun	Shemesh	Leo	Your Life's Purpose	To create, initiate, display, courage, self-expression, to shine
Moon	Levanah	Cancer	Your Physical, Emotional Needs	To receive, respond, nurture, sensitivity, mood, to reflect Sun
Mercury	Kokhav (Hama)	Gemini, Virgo	The Messenger	To learn, communicate
Venus	Kokhevet (Noga)	Taurus, Libra	The Lover	To acquire, relate
Mars	Ma'adim	Aries, Scorpio	The Warrior	To act, fight
Jupiter	Tzadek	Sagittarius, Pisces	The Sage	To explore, expand
Saturn	Shabtei	Capricorn, Aquarius	The Taskmaster	To be responsible
Uranus	Oron	Aquarius	The Revolutionary	To break with traditions
Neptune	Rahav	Pisces	The Dreamer	To seek out the divine
Pluto	n/a	Scorpio	The Transformer	To transform
Ascendant Ruler	According to Sign	Rising Sign	The Motivator	To guide course of your life

Interpreting Your Natal Chart
Start with your Sun Sign!

When you combine the functions of the Sun, the Moon and Rising Signs with each of their Signs and Triplicities, Quadruplicities and Polarities you can see how uniquely each person has been created! Each of these qualities is in a Zodiac Sign giving each Sign its own blend of characteristics.

How do these all work together? Here are the roles of each of the featured players in our Natal Charts.

The Sun in your Chart will indicate your nature, the core of your will, and the gifts and talents that will be used and developed as you go about doing your 'good works' as part of your life's purpose. (Ephesians 2:10).

The Moon in your Chart will reveal your physical and emotional needs that will be used and developed to fulfill your life's purpose.

The Rising Sign coordinates the entire Chart with the specific kind of outlook you have for living your life. It is called the 'Helm' of the Chart.

The Ruling Planet of the Rising Sign is called the 'Ruler' of the Chart. It is known as the 'Steersman' of the Helm of your Chart and shows the driving force behind how you function and operate in this world. It works together with your Sun Sign and Moon Sign to produce the personality that you use in the world to live your life and accomplish your purpose.

As you learn to blend each of the Luminaries and their characteristics you will understand the foundation of the building blocks of your personality. This blend is what makes your Star Pattern different from all others. The combination of their Modes,

Elements and Polarities give unique qualities to each of them. This is also known as synthesizing your Natal Chart. Synthesizing blends all the pieces together to come up with the perfect mix of YOU!

A suggested way to understand your Natal Chart and all the attributes it shows about your life and who you are, is to start learning about your Sun Sign, especially if you do not know your birth time. It is the Sign most people are aware of. There are no calculations required except to know their birthdate. Your attributes, as descried in your Sun Sign, reveal much about your identity, goals, and life's purpose. It represents your core traits and the way you shine.

As you read through your Sun Signs' characteristics, see which traits resonate with you and note the ones you see operating in your life. Reflect on the positive traits that each one represents. Let them sink into your heart and mind. Which ones are you strong in?

This will be quite an eye-opening experience if you have never had your Natal Chart interpreted and have not learned about the gifts and talents with which you were born. You will begin to discover characteristics of yourself that you did not know before. You will understand the reasons why you behave the way you do!

You will also be excited when you see gifts or talents you always thought you had but have remained hidden. When these traits are confirmed they can provide you with a vision to keep before your eyes that will help you press towards your goal. Your confidence will grow when you see the talent you thought you possessed actually confirmed on your Natal Chart. God really did give me this gift! You can then praise God knowing how closely He has been designing your life without you even knowing it!

Take some time to 'wear' the characteristics of the identity that are indicated by your Sun. When you learn about yourself in such an intimate way it will change your life. Let the newly discovered aspects of your identity sink in. It is important to seek the Lord through this time and let the Holy Spirit guide you through this discovery process.

After you understand more about your Sun Sign, you can study further the descriptions of your Moon and Rising Signs. They reveal more components of your unique personality. Following that, you can add the Sun's House and finally the Planet associated with your Rising Sign. You can take note of all these traits on the worksheet provided in the Chapter 'Interpreting Your Natal Chart.' Identify which of the them are already at work in your life.

Spiritually, the Sun, the Moon and the Rising Signs can be likened to the Spirit, Soul and Body respectively, or Will, Emotions, Mind. They are each separate, yet they operate together. They have individual characteristics and purposes, but their traits cannot always be defined exactly. They work together to accomplish the purpose for which you were created.

Some of the traits of the Luminaries will jump out at you and say, 'Yes, this is me!' Those are the traits to look at and determine if they are already working in your life. Have the events in your life made use of those traits? Do you want to improve them? If you have not experienced them yet, they can provide the vision to give direction to your life. You can get assurance that the dreams and desires you have are possible because God gave you the gifts and talents that you need to achieve them.

Write down key attributes that resonate with you on the worksheet that follows in the Chapter "Interpreting Your Natal Chart.'. Look at them periodically. Learn to identify them with yourself and build on them. Consider the traits that are available that you have yet to use. Can developing them help you accomplish more? Can they further your life vision? Can developing them help you to offset a behavior that is detrimental to your life?

The Sun, the Moon and the Rising Sign all work together. Another way to describe this interaction is, the Sun and the Sign it is in are what give you goals and direction to motivate your life, and the Moon position takes the needs and desires of your heart, your Sun, and works to fulfill them. They work together to accomplish their roles. This harmony is worked out during your life and gives you the tools you need to accomplish your purpose.

Here are a few simple illustrations using only the Sun, the Moon, and the Rising Sign as examples to show how the Luminaries all work together. They can work in harmony but there could also be some bumps in the road that can hinder this harmony.

Sun in Pisces and Moon in Leo - Leo's ego helps Pisces sacrificing nature, and the Sun's humble nature helps the Moon's pride. They can learn to balance each other.

Sun in Libra and Moon in Aries - Libra's peacemaking nature is opposed by Aries self-centered nature. There is an internal struggle as to which way to go, making decisions hard. Should I? Shouldn't I? Should I? Shouldn't I? Back and forth.

Sun in Capricorn and Rising Sign in Capricorn - The Rising Sign is in harmony with the Sun and both work together to develop and express the Sun's goal. Serious single-minded focus on achievement.

Sun in Taurus and Moon in Capricorn - Taurus' desire for the material is fed by Capricorn's drive to succeed. They both work together in a serious steady fashion to reach the top.

Sun in Scorpio and Moon in Aquarius - Deep probing Scorpio can be frustrated by Aquarius' non-committal emotions.

Sun in Leo and Moon in Leo - Sun (will) and Moon (emotions) compete for the spotlight. Goals and emotions are on the same path and can have intense expression.

These examples show the balance or inner struggles that may be present when you are trying to become whole. More Sign compatibilities are illustrated in the chapter on Compatibilities. The Sun is the psychological core that provides the foundation for your actions, your purpose, and the core interests of your life. It is the center of your life. The Sun represents the central purpose of your destiny. The Moon qualities help to fulfill it. The Rising Sign helps to orchestrate the purpose and presents it to the world.

For Believers, all these examples of the Luminary interactions are also spiritually intertwined with the Lord through the Holy Spirit, who helps us, especially when we cannot figure any of this out ourselves! They can be likened to interactions between our body, soul and spirit, or mind, will and emotions with the Holy Spirit's help to coordinate them all!

*I do not understand what I do. For what I want to do,
I do not do. But what I hate I do. Romans 7:15*

*In the same way, the Spirit helps us in our weakness. We do not
know what we ought to pray for, but the Spirit himself
intercedes for us through wordless groans. Romans 8:26*

Many issues take a lifetime to balance and bring to wholeness. It would be nice to be able to push a button and everything balances and reaches its full potential in harmony, but that is not how it happens. It seems as if we work out one issue in our lives and then a completely different one comes to the surface! We are truly a work in progress. And we have our time on Earth to work it all out!

It is as if we are born one way and then we have to spend our whole lives trying to become something else. Then we need to change and fix that! Sometimes we work on the same frustrating short comings of our personality all of our lives. This is just how it is.

Not everyone cares about improving themselves or trying to work on a problem before it gets out of control. Most people do not try to change anything unless the discomfort the problem trait causes in their lives becomes unbearable. Other people, especially spouses, almost force you to change in order to get along! This is why we need each other! Iron sharpens iron.

*As iron sharpens iron, so one person sharpens another.
Proverbs 27:17*

Thankfully, the Lord does have a pre-emptive plan for us, where we can work on one trait at a time, through the topics represented at the New Moon Celebrations each Month. This is where we get insight into how we are wired as revealed through our Natal Charts and find what is at the root of our issues and get solutions. With the Lord's help we will refine them so they align with His Love and we can become whole.

181

Putting it All Together
Four Elements times Three Modes equals Twelve Zodiac Signs!

$4 \times 3 = 12$

There are twelve Signs each representing twelve basic human natures. These come from a combination of the four Elements, the three modes and the two polarities. These combinations make up the characteristics displayed by each of the twelve Signs of the Zodiac. They each describe a facet of our basic human nature.

Let us put them together to see what your unique Sun Sign combination is! Following is a summary of the components that give each Zodiac Sign its unique characteristics.

Signs, Modes (Quadruplicities), Elements (Triplicities), Polarities (Dualities)

Spring

Aries: Cardinal, Fire/Choleric, Masculine
Leading, Energy/passion, Initiating
Taurus: Fixed, Earth/Melancholic, Feminine
Stabilizing, Material/values, Receptive
Gemini: Mutable, Air/Sanguine, Masculine
Adaptable, Communication/thought, Initiating

Summer

Cancer: Cardinal, Water/Phlegmatic, Feminine
Leading, Emotions/Intuition, Receptive
Leo: Fixed, Fire/Choleric, Masculine
Stabilizing, Energy/Passion, Initiating
Virgo: Mutable, Earth/Melancholic, Feminine
Adaptable, Material/Values, Receptive

Fall

Libra: Cardinal, Air/Sanguine, Masculine
Leading, Intellect/Communication, Initiating
Scorpio: Fixed, Water, Feminine
Stabilizing, Emotion/Intuition, Receptive
Sagittarius: Mutable, Fire, Masculine
Adaptable, Energy/Passion, Initiating

Winter

Capricorn: Cardinal, Earth, Feminine
Leading, Material/Values, Receptive
Aquarius: Fixed, Air, Masculine
Stabilizing, Intellect/Communication, Initiating
Pisces: Mutable, Water, Feminine
Changeable, Emotions/Intuition, Receptive

Signs

♈ Aries	♋ Cancer	♎ Libra	♑ Capricorn
♉ Taurus	♌ Leo	♏ Scorpio	♒ Aquarius
♊ Gemini	♍ Virgo	♐ Sagittarius	♓ Pisces

Duality

Masculine

Feminine

Triplicity

Fire

Earth

Air

Water

Quadruplicity

Cardinal

Fixed

Mutable

The Zodiacal Signs Ruler	Principle	Keywords
♈ ARIES........... Mars	I Am..............	Motivated to act.............
♉ TAURUS........ Venus	I Have...........	Practical & persevering.
♊ GEMINI......... Mercury	I Think..........	Duality. Communicative.
♋ CANCER....... Moon	I Feel............	Emotional & nurturing.....
♌ LEO............... Sun	I Will.............	Desires recognition........
♍ VIRGO.......... Mercury	I Analyze......	Attention to detail..........
♎ LIBRA........... Venus	I Balance......	Relates to others...........
♏ SCORPIO..... Mars/Pluto	I Desire.........	Intense & forceful...........
♐ SAGITTARIUS Jupiter	I Aspire.....	Broad outlook, idealistic.
♑ CAPRICORN. Saturn	I Use.............	Realistic & responsible...
♒ AQUARIUS... Saturn/Uranus	I Know..........	Human understanding....
♓ PISCES......... Jupiter/Neptune	I Believe.......	Spiritual & sensitive........

The Planets & Personal Points

☉	SUN..............	Spirit, life force & identity. Masculine principle
☽	MOON..........	Soul, emotions, and instincts. Domesticity. Feminine principle
☿	MERCURY....	Intellect and power of communication. The reasoning mind
♀	VENUS........	Love, beauty, art, and attraction
♂	MARS...........	Energy, action, aggression, and conflict
♃	JUPITER.......	Wisdom, expansion, optimism & success
♄	SATURN........	Restriction, limitation, restraint & sorrow
♅	URANUS.......	Change, originality, revolution & eccentricity
♆	NEPTUNE.....	Imagination, spirituality, inspiration, illusion & deception
♇	PLUTO..........	Power, forces beyond personal control & transformation
Aˢ	ASCENDANT.	Face you show the world. Primary motivation in life

The Houses

1st	HOUSE	Physical appearance, self-expression, and vitality
2nd	HOUSE	Personal assets, wealth and earning ability
3rd	HOUSE	Immediate environment, siblings, mentality and communication
4th	HOUSE	Home, family, origins, father, and later life
5th	HOUSE	Pleasures, amusements, love & children
6th	HOUSE	Service, work & health
7th	HOUSE	Partners, other people generally & open enemies
8th	HOUSE	Other people's resources, wills, legacies & death
9th	HOUSE	Long journeys, higher learning, religion, and law
10th	HOUSE	Reputation, career & the mother
11th	HOUSE	Friends, benefactors, and groups
12th	HOUSE	Self-undoing, withdrawal, retreat, and seclusion

The Components of each Zodiac Sign

Triplicities

Element/Temperament	Nature	Characteristics
Fire/Choleric	Energy	Passionate, active, courageous
Earth/Melancholic	Material	Practical, down to Earth, materialistic
Air/Sanguine	Intellect	Intellectual, sensible, logical
Water/Phlegmatic	Emotions	Emotional, intuitive, sensitive

Quadruplicities

Mode of Operation	Nature	Method of Actions
Cardinal	Leading	Outgoing, initiating
Fixed	Stable	Rigid opinions, security oriented
Mutable	Changeable	Flexible and adaptable.

Polarities

Duality	Elements	Initiating or Receptive
Masculine	Fire and Air	Active, initiating, positive
Feminine	Earth and Water	Passive, receptive, negative

Your Unique Combination

Here is where you can begin to combine the components of your Primary Star Pattern and get to know the characteristics with which you were born! If you do not know all of your components yet, you can get your Natal Chart information at www.YourDestinyDiscovered.com.

My date, time, place of birth: _____ _____ _____

My Primary Star Pattern (Fill in your Natal Chart information):

My **Sun** (my will) is in the Sign of _____

My **Moon** (my emotions) is in the Sign of _____

My **Rising Sign** (persona) is _____

My **Sun** is in the # _____House (where my Sun shines)

My **Chart's Ruling Planet** (my main motivation) is _____

Details of my Primary Star Pattern:
Using the tables and descriptions provided in the preceding pages, fill in the following with the key characteristics:

My Sun is in the Sign of _____

My Sun Sign's Mode: (circle)   Cardinal   Fixed   Mutable
My Sun Sign's Element: (circle)   Fire   Earth   Air   Water
My Sun Sign's Polarity: (circle)   Masculine   Feminine

The expression of the gifts and talents at core of my Sun, (my will and creativity) are:

_____
List keywords for the traits of your Sun's Mode

_____
List keywords for the traits of your Sun's Element

_____
List the keywords for the traits of your Sun's Polarity

188

The area in which I need to use and develop my Sun's potential is: (Enter the House number shown in your Natal Chart)

My Sun is in the #_____ HOUSE of_____

_____

List the House number and the keywords for the area of life represented by the House your Sun occupies

My Moon is in the Sign of _____

My Moon Sign's Mode: (circle)   Cardinal   Fixed   Mutable
My Moon Sign's Element: (circle)   Fire   Earth   Air   Water
My Moon Sign's Polarity: (circle)   Masculine   Feminine

The way my emotional and security (Moon's) needs are reflected:

_____

List keywords for the traits of your Moon's Mode

_____

List keywords for the traits of your Moon's Element

_____

List keywords for the traits of your Moon's Polarity

The way I project and process my life is shown through my Rising Sign:

My Rising Sign is _____

My Rising Sign's Mode: (circle)   Cardinal   Fixed   Mutable
My Rising Sign's Element: (circle)   Fire   Earth   Air   Water
My Rising Sign's Polarity: (circle)   Masculine   Feminine

_____

List keywords for the traits of your Rising Sign's Mode

_____

List keywords for the traits of your Rising Sign's Element

_____

List the keywords for the traits of your Rising Sign's Polarity

The Ruling Planet of my Chart - overall motivation of life:

The Ruling Planet of my Chart is: _____
(Enter the Planet associated with your Rising Sign)

_____
List the keywords of your Ruling Planet, its motivating impulse

Another way to say it...
The Summary of My Unique Star Pattern:

Fill in your Sun, Moon, Rising Sign, Sun's House, and Ruling Planet
and then write a sentence about each.

The primary impulse of my life is shown by the Ruling Planet:
List **Ruling Planet**: _____

_____Wri
te a sentence describing how your Ruling Planet provides the primary
impulse of your life.

My will shines through my Sun Sign:

List your **Sun Sign**:_____

_____
Write a sentence describing how your will shines through your Sun
Sign's characteristics

My Sun is used and developed in the House of the Sun:
List the **House** your Sun occupies in your Natal Chart:

_____

_____
Write a sentence describing how your Sun is used and developed
through the House your Sun is in

My Sun is refined by my emotions as reflected in my Moon Sign:

My Moon Sign is: _____

_____
Write a sentence describing how your Moon Sign works together with your Sun Sign characteristics

*My outward **personality** is display by my **Rising Sign**:*

My Rising Sign is: _____

_____
Write a sentence describing how your personality is displayed by your Rising Sign's characteristics

Write out sentences combining the various qualities of the components of your Primary Star Pattern. Identify the traits you see working strongly in your life, the ones that you are having trouble with, and others that you want to use and develop more.

As you go through each day, you will see confirmations of the traits you have written here that will verify that your Mazal is real!

Your Natal Chart Grows Along with You

The position of the Luminaries, which are The Sun, The Moon and The Stars, on the day of your birth show you the qualities at the beginning of your life. You can see the potentials and pitfalls, and you can learn to work them out. Some of your traits are developed early in life. Some come about later. Even so, these characteristics are a part of your life from the very beginning.

Each experience of life builds upon the qualities with which you were born and makes you even more unique. Even if people are twins, they are not born exactly at the same moment, which makes their Charts different to the extent that their birth times differ. In addition, from the moment they are born, they will have different life experiences, which they interpret and internalize in their own way and form them into their unique personality. Every person is born with free will, which ensures that no two people will have the exact same experiences in life.

Some people may identify themselves strongly with their Sun Sign, and do not recognize the other components of their personality. When you learn the traits of the Moon and Rising Signs you can integrate them with the traits of your Sun Sign. You can identify your strongest traits and use them to help overcome and then strengthen the weaker traits.

You may have one trait that is the hardest for you to get under control. It is like a thorn in the flesh that you cannot get rid of. You can identify other strengths you have and use them to help overcome that trait. Many times, we need God's help to accomplish a difficult change in a character trait. Prayer, praise, and study of the Word are big factors in being able to overcome problem areas and bring peace and balance to your life. (2 Corinthians 12:6-9).

You may come across some seemingly inconsistent traits when synchronizing, or when putting together each of the characteristics of your Luminaries. This is because each characteristic is also impacted by the position of the other eight Planets in your Natal Chart. These Planets will modify the Luminary's expression. These Planets can add their own desirable or undesirable quality to the mix. This will provide a more advanced interpretation, which you can add when you are ready to study the additional components of your Natal Chart.

There are books about Astrology listed in the Bibliography that can support your continued studies, should you have an interest to do so. But no matter what the other combinations or variations are, the underlying influence of your Sun Sign will be operating and that is the focus of the introductory material in this book.

Keep an open mind and see which attributes resonate with your life. Seek the Lord for His guidance. You will not display every trait listed for each of your Zodiac Signs because other factors in your Natal Chart will add or detract from the expression of the listed traits.

You are unique. You have varying amounts and different expressions of the traits found in your Primary Star Pattern. You can ask the Lord to develop the positive traits you resonate with and to remove or lessen the destructive traits. Remember, this is a wonderful lifelong process and journey! You will learn more about yourself and the Lord every day and will continue to be amazed.

Astrology is an Art that takes time to develop and fully understand. If you start with your Sun Sign alone, and learn its qualities, you will understand a great deal about yourself and your life's purpose. As you study, learn, and pray about your Blueprint in the Heavens you will gain even deeper understanding. Ask the Holy Spirit to reveal to you new revelations about your Natal Chart, especially when you are going through challenging times. There are new insights available when you need them! For further help with the interpretation of the rest of your Natal Chart, a Faith-based Astrologer can help you understand it and give you greater insight.

Compatibility Among the Signs
How We Get Along with Ourselves and Others

Which Signs work and communicate easily together and which Signs have difficulty? Based on the makeup of each of the Zodiac Signs we can get an indication of the compatibility of the Signs. Keep in mind that one incompatible Sign does not make an incompatible relationship. There are many factors in every person's Chart and any one of those can offset any incompatibility shown in these examples. That being said, here are some compatibility combinations that can be used to help understand yourself and those around you in a relationship. You can compare your Sun, Moon, and Rising Sign to the Sun, the Moon, and the Rising Sign of the other person.

Signs in the Same Zodiac Sign

Luminaries in the same Zodiac Sign work well together and intensify each other. Together, their energies are focused and blended together. This compatibility is good but sometimes there is too much of a good thing. Planets in the same Sign have the same Modality, Element and Polarity. Being so alike may cause imbalance with either too much of a positive trait or too much of a bad trait. What was a good trait may become difficult to handle.

Signs with the Same Element

If both Signs are of the same Element, they are the most compatible. These are Signs with the same Elements but have different Modalities (Cardinal, Fixed, Mutable.) All the Fire Signs generally get along well with the other Fire Signs, the Earth with the other Earth Signs, the Air with the other Air Signs and the Water with the other Water signs. If two people are both in the exact same Sign, see above!

The energy flows seamlessly between the Signs with the same Element. Sometimes it can be so seamless that it can lead to laziness. Their gifts and talents can be encouraged and developed together. When there are opportunities to use them, they will flow in great harmony.

These Signs with the same Element are generally the most compatible.

The **Fire Signs** compatible with other **Fire Signs** are Aries, Leo, and Sagittarius

The **Earth Signs** compatible with other **Earth Signs** are Taurus, Virgo, and Capricorn

The **Air Signs** compatible with other **Air Signs** are Gemini, Libra, and Aquarius

The **Water Signs** compatible with other **Water Signs** are Cancer, Scorpio, and Pisces

Signs with the Same Polarity

The energy flow between Signs that are of the same polarity, being either **both Masculine or both being Feminine**, creates a very cooperative environment. Fire and Air are naturally complimentary and the same is true for Earth and Water. Signs with the same Polarity, or duality, are those which naturally work well together. They do well with each other when combined in the correct proportions.

Each of the Sign's traits inspire and encourage the other's traits and they do not hold each other back. They are able to collaborate and work well together. New ideas and opportunities can flow smoothly between different areas of life. These Elements provide a balanced approach to life and are well rounded, flexible, and adaptable. This compatibility allows outlooks and ideas to flow easily between the two Signs.

These are the odd and even numbered Signs of the Zodiac, which get along with the other odd or even numbered Signs.

These Signs with the same Polarity are generally compatible.

The **Fire Signs**
Aries, Leo, and Sagittarius are compatible
with the **Air Signs**
Gemini, Libra, and Aquarius

The **Earth Signs**
Taurus, Virgo, and Capricorn are compatible
with the **Water Signs**
of Cancer, Scorpio, and Pisces

Signs with the Same Modalities - Difficult yet Productive

Signs that have the same modality have only the modality in common and nothing else.

They DO share the Modes, or Quadruplicities
of Cardinal, Fixed, or Mutable.

They **DO NOT have** any of the **same Elements** and their **Polarities** are different.

These Signs are not compatible, and they do not complement one another. They are individuals with different personalities resulting in unstable relationships. They represent opposing types of temperaments. The relationship between these Signs creates restrictions and obstacles.

However, in a positive light, because of the conflicts the Signs can push each other to integrate and force each other to grow. This difficulty can spur them on and cause them to be productive. This is not easy and can lead to frustration and irritation during the process. Unless the desire or necessity is there, the relationship may not be successful. There are many changes that need to be made, but the end result will help the individuals develop and grow.

The Signs and those with which they are likely to have conflict, tension, and power struggles:

Aries: Cancer, Capricorn
Taurus: Leo, Aquarius
Gemini: Virgo, Pisces
Cancer: Libra, Aries
Leo: Scorpio, Taurus
Virgo: Sagittarius, Gemini

Libra: Capricorn, Cancer
Scorpio: Aquarius, Leo
Sagittarius: Pisces, Virgo
Capricorn: Aries, Libra
Aquarius: Taurus, Scorpio
Pisces: Gemini, Sagittarius

Opposing Signs

Signs that are directly opposite to each other on the Zodiac Wheel are likely to experience deep tension.

Even though they are of the **same Modality and Polarity** they are of **different Elements**.

These Elements would normally be compatible, but the standoff between the same Modality and Polarity make it just that - a standoff! These signs oppose each other and manifest as a kind of duality - where one side must cooperate and give something up or else break.

Many times, the energies of the Planets in these aspects end up providing the core experiences of life that cause change and growth.

As an example, this can result in the challenging basis of marriage. One partner is naturally represented in the First House of Self and the other partner is represented directly across from them in the Seventh House of Marriage and Partnership. They are designed to oppose each other in their relationship. No wonder it can be challenging! This opposition can lead to frustration when not integrated, but through hard work, a balance of opposite Signs can be achieved. They work hard to reach compromise and balance, and each change in the process.

These opposite Signs have challenging compatibility:

Aries Libra
Taurus - Scorpio
Gemini - Sagittarius
Cancer - Capricorn
Leo - Aquarius
Virgo - Pisces

Libra- Aries
Scorpio - Taurus
Sagittarius - Gemini
Capricorn - Cancer
Aquarius - Leo
Pisces - Virgo

Signs of different Modality, Elements and Polarities

The compatibility issue for these Signs is, "They don't understand each other." They are of different Modality, different Element, and different Polarity. They have little in common and have quite different styles and outlooks on life. It is not so much the negative, but the indifference that brings strain to the relationship. For compatibility they will need to compartmentalize certain areas of their lives, keeping them separate, in order to get along. They have different agendas and these relationships will require continual compromise.

The Signs with little in common and low compatibility.

Aries: Scorpio, Pisces
Taurus: Libra, Sagittarius
Gemini: Scorpio, Capricorn
Cancer: Sagittarius, Aquarius
Leo: Capricorn, Pisces
Virgo: Aquarius, Aries

Libra: Pisces, Taurus
Scorpio: Aries, Gemini
Sagittarius: Taurus, Cancer
Capricorn: Gemini, Leo
Aquarius: Cancer, Virgo
Pisces: Leo, Libra

Neutral Signs - Signs next to each other on the Zodiac Wheel

These Signs are adjacent to each other in the Zodiac Wheel. Although they do not have common components, they are mildly compatible with each other due to their proximity. These Signs work together with slight discomfort and share minor opportunities and resources.

Slight compatibility between Sign of close proximity.

Aries: Taurus, Pisces
Taurus: Aries, Gemini
Gemini: Taurus, Cancer
Cancer: Gemini, Leo
Leo: Cancer, Virgo
Virgo: Leo, Libra

Libra: Virgo, Scorpio
Scorpio: Libra, Sagittarius
Sagittarius: Scorpio, Capricorn
Capricorn: Sagittarius, Aquarius
Aquarius: Capricorn, Pisces
Pisces: Aquarius, Aries

Remember when viewing all of these combinations, we are comparing only single factors of the Chart. It does not provide an ample basis to determine whether or not the entire relationship is compatible or challenged. But it does give interesting and useful insight into issues the Signs may have with each other.

We must always remember that God puts people together, and the challenges they face are for their ultimate growth. Regardless of the Signs involved, issues can and will be worked out if the relationships are of Him. He is, and we are, above the Planets!

Concerning the physical Elements that are not as compatible as the others, there is an interesting scientific reaction that happens with changes in temperature. Temperature plays an important role in how the atoms react and change when heated up or cooled down.

Depending on the temperature, the physical Elements can themselves be changed, and they can change each other. Water can become ice or steam. Fire can melt Earth/ore and make steel. Fire can temper Earth/clay and hardens pottery. Cold Water can put out a hot Fire. Controlling the temperature can limit or expand their effects on each other.

In the same way, our personalities can be tempered by changing our 'temperature.' We can get along with others even when we have incompatible parts of our personalities. We can change our personalities from cold to hot and hot to cold. Granted, to change our personality temperaments is not as easy as changing the temperature of physical Elements, but with time, effort, and prayer we are able to refine and adapt.

Continual application of the Word of God in our lives can change our temperaments and over time the evidence will be displayed. The Word of God speaks about the 12 fruits of the Spirit. As we are tempered by the Word of God, our elemental temperatures can be adjusted making even seemingly incompatible Elements get along!

According to Galatians 5:22, the 12 Fruits of the Spirit are love, joy, peace, patience, kindness, goodness, long-suffering, gentleness, faith, modesty, self-control, and chastity. As we grow in the manifestation of these fruits, we become more compatible and adaptable both with ourselves and with others!

AN IMPORTANT WORD

Astrology is a Divine Science

However, Caution is Needed for Believers!

If you want to study more on your own, you need to prepare yourself for the terminology and concepts you will come across that conflict with Biblical Truths and Born-again Christian Beliefs.

My mission, as directed by the Lord, is to present the Heavens according to the principles and beliefs found in the Bible, and in the Ancient Hebrew writings, to Born-again Believers who want to learn more about their life and purpose through their Mazal, or Natal Chart. The amount of insight received from an interpretation of a person's Mazal through the Divine Science of Astrology, is life changing and many people want to learn more about this amazing science. However, a word of caution for the Believer is needed.

If you want to delve into learning more about Astrology and discover more about yourself and your gifts, talents, and purpose, you will discover that there are only a very few books written with the Born-again Christian, Believing in the One True God, version of Astrology available. This is why the Lord instructed me to write this book!

This book, *Your Destiny Discovered, Astrology for Believers,* provides an introductory teaching on the Luminaries, the Heavenly Lights, from a Biblical perspective. It is meant to get you started on the path to interpreting your Natal Chart leading to the discovery of your true identity!

While this book gives you the information you need to begin your journey, there is much more to learn. However, if you want to study more, you will need to read books that are not written from a 'religious' viewpoint.

In order to learn more about Astrology using other sources you will need to prepare yourself for the terminology and concepts that we as Born-again Believers have been taught to avoid. You will need to read some secular books to get the basic scientific information and from there you can interpret the information from God's viewpoint.

You will also find much information on Astrology from a Kabbalistic esoteric viewpoint. While we do get a significant amount of information from Kabbalah that helps us grow closer to God and understand the Heavens, it also uses some terminology and presents beliefs that are not consistent with the Born-again viewpoint. Their view on the timing of the coming of the Messiah and whether His coming will be the first or the second time is one example.

When reading secular books, it is important to be strong in your knowledge of the Word of God so you will be able to discern what does not agree with Biblical truth. It is important to ask the Lord to protect you and guide you as you study. Pray for discernment before each study session.

When encountering the New Age words and concepts you will find in many Astrology books, you must learn to substitute the original meaning from the Ancient Biblical text. Assign back to them the meaning the Word of God gives them. Most of the time the concept for the word itself started with a Biblical meaning and was then corrupted to suit those who wanted to take the religion out of Astrology. It is important to return it to the original meaning that agrees with the Word of God.

The abundance of New Age terminology will deter many Believers from studying Astrology. You do not need to study Astrology extensively. You can get a personal interpretation from a Faith-based Astrologer that will give you what you need to know without having to study for years. The study of Astrology is like preparing to become a doctor. There are a lot of details and idiosyncrasies, and practice is needed. The ability to interpret the Blueprint of the Heavens is what makes it an Art. To make it a profession is not for everyone. But the information is there for anyone.

For those who do want to learn more, here are examples of common terms I have discovered which are contrary concepts to our Biblical understanding, and their Biblical substitutions. You will not come across some of these very often, but when you do it is important to know what they mean and if there is a Biblical equivalent. Understand the original meanings and relate them back to the Biblical fundamentals from which they came.

New Age Term = Biblical Fundamental Meaning

Karma = Sowing and Reaping, you reap what you sow.

"Do not be deceived: God cannot be mocked. A man reaps what he sows. Whoever sows to please their flesh, from the flesh will reap destruction; whoever sows to please the Spirit, from the Spirit will reap eternal life. Let us not become weary in doing good, for at the proper time we will reap a harvest if we do not give up". Galatians 6:7-9

Reincarnation = Christian Born-again theology does not agree with the reincarnation teaching. However, if reincarnation were true, the Bible teaches that Yeshua paid the price for all of our sins and mistakes, in this lifetime or any other. Once we have accepted Him as our Savior, we do not have to do works to pay our debt anymore. All has been forgiven. This is the last stop before life in Heaven with Him for all eternity. Our 'karmic' debt has been paid by Yeshua! Jesus!

And just as each person is destined to die once and after that comes judgment... Hebrews 9:27

But he was pierced for our transgressions, he was crushed for
our iniquities; the punishment that brought us peace
was on him, and by his wounds we are healed.
We all, like sheep, have gone astray, each of us has turned to
our own way; and the LORD has laid on him
the iniquity of us all. Isaiah 53:5-6

For the wages of sin is death, but the gift of God is
eternal life in Christ Jesus our Lord.
Romans 6:23

For God so loved the world that he gave his one and only Son,
that whoever believes in him shall not perish but have eternal
life. For God did not send his Son into the world to condemn the
world, but to save the world through him.
John 3:16

Higher Self = We are seated with Messiah on His throne at the right hand of the Father, HIGH above all else. We are to grow in His likeness. This is our "higher self," the likeness fashioned after Yeshua, and His LOVE! We are not gods, yet we are seated with God Almighty in Heavenly places. Therefore, we strive to be all that we can be for Him. We are told to be like Him, but not to be Him.

And God raised us up with Christ and seated us with him in the
heavenly realms in Christ Jesus. Ephesians 2:6

Therefore, since you have been raised with Christ, strive for the
things above, where Christ is seated at the right hand of God.
Set your minds on things above, not on earthly
things. Colossians 3:1-2

Yin-Yang = Negative-Positive, Feminine-Masculine. There are two sides that complement each other such as light and dark, male, and female, Sun, and Moon. It describes polarity. Yin is inward energy, passive, feminine, receptive, negative, cold, and dark. Yang is outward energy, active, masculine, aggressive, positive, hot, and light. The world is fundamentally balanced in positive and negative.

Spirit Guide = Holy Spirit. While we only have access to the Holy Spirit of God through Salvation, there are other spirits who convey information to man from the spirit realm. Stay away from any counterfeit spirit guides that are not directly associated with the God of Abraham, Isaac, and Jacob through Yeshua our Savior. Seek the voice of the true Holy Spirit when you are studying and let Him guide you.

But when he, the Spirit of truth, comes, he will guide you into all the truth. He will not speak on his own; he will speak only what he hears, and he will tell you what is yet to come.
John 16:13

So I say, let the Holy Spirit guide your lives. Then you won't be doing what your sinful nature craves.
Galatians 5:15 NLT

Channeling = Make sure you are tuned in to the right 'channel' that is connected to the God of Abraham, Isaac, and Jacob. Always test the spirits and make sure they are of God. The Christian faith does not consult the dead. They consult only the One True and Living God.

When someone tells you to consult mediums and spiritists, who whisper and mutter, should not a people inquire of their God? Why consult the dead on behalf of the living? Consult God's instruction and the testimony of warning. If anyone does not speak according to this word, they have no light of dawn. Isaiah 8:1-20

Dear friends, do not believe every spirit, but test the spirits to see whether they are from God, because many false prophets have gone out into the world. This is how you can recognize the Spirit of God: Every spirit that acknowledges that Jesus Christ has come in the flesh is from God, but every spirit that does not acknowledge Jesus is not from God. This is the spirit of the antichrist, which you have heard is coming and even now is already in the world. 1 John 4:1-3

In your studies, if you feel uncomfortable while reading new information, stop reading. Seek the Lord as to what Biblical meaning could be behind it if there is one. Is it compatible with what you already know based on Biblical principles? If you do not find the concept compatible with your beliefs and doctrines, reject it and move on. You do not need to accept anything that does not line up with Scripture, both written and oral. You do not want or need to read everything that is available.

It is important to note that there are good books written by secular Astrologers that teach the components of Astrology. References for some helpful books are listed in the Bibliography at the end of this book. You will learn much from these writings. The understanding, interpretation, and application of the information are where you need to be sure to apply Biblical principles.

Ask the Holy Spirit to guide you as to what to read and to give you a reverent understanding of this Ancient science of Astrology, the Divine Science when you study.

Not everyone needs to become an Astrologer, but the time has come for Believers to become familiar with the basics in order to follow the Signs of the Times as seen in the Heavens and to strengthen themselves and their walk Lord.

More Faith-based Astrologers are needed to minister to their fellow Believers. Believers have nowhere to go except New Age Astrologers at this point. Astrology is a necessary tool and it is of vital importance that Kingdom Believers, Kings and Priests, rise up as they are called to help other Believers discover their Kingdom Identity and help them get the answers for which they are searching. **More Faith-based Astrologers are needed to help people discover their gifts and talents now!**

New Moon Celebrations

The Significance of the New Moon in Our Lives

Everywhere on Earth, all Nations, all people, share the same Stars in the Heavens. All people groups have developed their unique stories and have given their meanings to the Zodiac and the signs in the Heavens. Only one faith acknowledges that the Sun, the Moon, and the Stars are servants of the One True God and are not gods themselves. This is the Jewish faith. For Gentiles, this is the faith of Abraham, Isaac, and Jacob through Yeshua ha Mashiach, Jesus the Messiah, through Whom we are grafted in.

When we, as Believers, think of the Planets and the other Heavenly bodies that are present in the space between our world and the Throne of God, we must see them as did Abraham and our forefathers in the faith and be like them to give all the glory to God.

The Sun, the Moon and the Stars are Biblical timers that were set into place by God at Creation (Genesis 1:4). They each have their purpose and place in God's time cycles. They provide a system of timekeeping that, according to His calendar is different from the secular Julian or Gregorian calendars.

The Moon in particular is intimately involved with God's holy calendar that helps guide our lives. The timing of the observances of the Feasts and Festivals of the Lord as recorded in the Book of Exodus, are based on the phases of the Moon. Each New Moon help us to number our days and to mark the passage of time. (Psalm 104:19; Psalm 90:12) The directive and tradition to observe the new Month in Exodus 12:2 identified it as a time to rejoice, dedicate the New Month to the Lord, and to seek His guidance both corporately and individually (Numbers 10:10).

While we are to be in constant daily communication with God through the Holy Spirit, He asks us to also meet with Him at regularly scheduled times. These times are the yearly Feast and Festivals. He also desires a scheduled meeting with us each Month. He sets an appointment for us to officially check in with Him every New Moon.

"...From one New Moon to another and from one Sabbath to another, all mankind will come and bow down before me," says the Lord. Isaiah 66:23

In Biblical times, the New Moon was observed by the Patriarchs of our faith as well as the Priests, and Prophets as they served the Lord. However, this observance has not yet been accepted by the Church in general or the Born-again Believers individually. Most are not even aware it exists. The significance of this important timepiece has been lost for centuries, leaving an alarming number of people who are in or out of the Church unaware of the amazing insights for their lives the Moon can provide. As a consequence, they search unceasingly for information about their identity and purpose, never getting the full picture.

The good news is that the tools that God has provided for Believers to find these answers are making a comeback. They include the rich heritage of the Biblical Feasts and Festivals, as well as the Sabbath. These have been discovered by many Believers over the past 50 years. Recently the richness of the New Moon is also being discovered by a number of Believers.

The Lord has designed His calendar, which includes the New Moons, for us to discover more of our purpose and destiny. Each New Moon is unique in its meaning and teaching and holds insight into God and His plan for our lives.

As we flow with God's calendar it helps us recognize and develop our gifts and talents. It helps us see and transform our shortcomings. As we align with His cycles, plans, and timing, we become more aware of our lives and purpose in God's great plan.

The Sun and the Moon each have a purpose and they are tools to be used at this time by God's children to live in victory and harmony with Him. One day the Sun and the Moon will be no more.

In his days may the righteous flourish and prosperity abound till the Moon is no more. Psalm 72:7

One day we will live by the Light of the Lord,

The Sun will no more be your light by day, nor will the brightness of the Moon shine on you, for the LORD will be your everlasting light, and your God will be your glory. Your Sun will never set again, and your Moon will wane no more; the LORD will be your everlasting light, and your days of sorrow will end. Isaiah 16:19-20

Until then, we are asked to live and learn with the Lights He has given us, the Sun, and the Moon, both physically and spiritually. The Moon is a faithful witness to the presence of God in our lives.

Once for all, I have sworn by my holiness— and I will not lie to David— that his line will continue forever and his throne endure before me like the Sun; it will be established forever like the Moon, the faithful witness in the sky. Psalm 89:35-38

The time has come for Born-again Believers, Christians, Believers in Yeshua ha Mashiach, the One New Man, to fully utilize the cycles of God. We need to learn to see the Heavens as Adam and Eve did, as a way God uses to communicate with His children on an intimate basis. It is time to bring back the observation of the New Moon and discover the rich messages God displays in the Heavens each Month.

The revelations that each New Moon provides for us during this special time with the Lord will open a new understanding of God's ways which we as, Believers, have not seen before. It will deepen our walk with the Lord and give us the victory we seek. It will change our lives one Month at a time!

12 Months to Wholeness

Heaven's Discipleship Program

Each Month is designed to help you understand more about the person God created you to be. Each Month is unique in God's calendar. As previously discussed, there are many themes and meanings associated with each Month and the number 12, so many that we personally cannot focus and study each one every Month. We need to be led by the Spirit as to which ones to highlight and glean from for any particular Month.

Each Month generally includes a study of the traditional meanings of that particular Month which often include a Feast and Festival. These studies are based on the traditional meanings that have been passed down from Scripture, the Sages, and from science and tradition as well as its spiritual and prophetic meanings. These meanings will teach you more about God. They will build the foundation of your relationship with Him.

Each Month there is also a specific area of life the Lord wants us all to learn more about and bring it into alignment with Him. *Each* of the twelve Months represents one of the 12 general areas of life that are common to man. These areas are described by the 12 Signs and Houses in the Zodiac Wheel, also called the Wheel of Life. The New Moon shows us which area of life is the focus for that Month.

General Life Areas
To find what the current Month's focus is we look at which Sign of the Zodiac the Moon is in when it aligns with the Sun that Month. This is the New MOON. (The New MONTH on the Hebrew

calendar begins a few days later when the crescent of the New Moon is visible to the naked eye.) The location of the New Moon in the Zodiac indicates the topic that is in focus for the world for that Month. This is the area of life that everyone who is in tune with the timings of God will reflect on. We can all receive insight and answers about our lives and personality by seeking God's insight into the Month's specific topic.

Following are the general areas of life that we can all can gain insight into each New Moon:

New Moon

Zodiac - Hebrew Month	House - Area of Life
Aries - Nissan	1 - Identity, Image, Self
Taurus - Iyar	2 - Possessions, Value, Worth, Money
Gemini - Sevan	3 - Communication, Knowledge, Siblings, Logic
Cancer - Tammuz	4 - Family (Parents), Security, Home
Leo - Av	5 - Pleasure, Creativity, Children, Fun
Virgo - Elul	6 - Health, Service, Work
Libra - Tishrei	7 - Marriage, Relationships, Unions
Scorpio - Cheshvan	8 - Death, Transformation, Power, Sex, Psychology
Sagittarius - Kislev	9 - Philosophy, Beliefs, Ethics, Travel
Capricorn - Tevet	10 - Social, Career, Authority
Aquarius - Shevat	11 - Friendship, Community, Hope
Pisces - Adar	12 - Spirituality, Solitude, Self-reflection

You can find the specific characteristics of the Signs and Houses in the earlier chapters of this book to gain more insight as to their meaning and how these meanings apply to your world.

As you follow God's cycle throughout the year, you will take a look at every major area of your life at each New Moon and seek ways to align it with the Lord. Every Month, as the Lord reveals His insight and blessings, you will grow in wisdom, knowledge and understanding.

Specific Focus

Once you have had your Natal Chart cast and know your Rising Sign, you will be able to pinpoint the specific area of life that will be in focus for you that Month. The area of focus for you individually is based on which House the New Moon falls in your Natal Chart. This is shown by the Sign the New Moon is in that Month.

Where the New Moon falls in your Chart is like a pointer pointing to the area of life that you are directed to focus your attention. When studying the meaning of the New Moon in your personal Chart, it is not so much the Sign the Moon is in, but the House in which it falls. The topics of the House where the Moon is in your Chart will be the area of personal study and reflection that Month.

For example, if the New Moon is in Aries and you have the Sign of Aries in your Fifth House, the area of life represented by the Fifth House will be the one to focus on that Month. The Moon is 'pointing' to that area. Then you would seek the Lord as to what He would have you discover about your Fifth House, which deals with creativity, children, ego, romance, speculation, and any gifts and talents you have associated with them. You will pray to see if there is anything more you need to learn about or need to align with the Lord in that area of your life.

Each Month we are asked to seek the Lord and His insight, correction, and direction for the part of life that the New Moon represents for us. This helps us grow and develop the gifts and talents with which we were born so we can fulfill His purpose for our lives. This discipline adds to our spiritual, mental, and physical growth.

How to Celebrate the New Moon

The New Moon is a powerful time to meet with the Lord. It is a time to dedicate the Month to Him as well as get direction for our lives. Its roots go back to creation, but it is just now being reborn, being discovered by Believers for the first time.

Taking the time to celebrate each New Moon provides a greater understanding of life and purpose in God's great plan. It is an evolving feast of the Lord.

Some **suggested** guidelines as to how to observe the New Moon are found in the Bible. Much is also contained in the Jewish Oral and Written Law that has not yet been discovered by many Gentile Believers. Much of the actual detail is open to interpretation, requiring Believers to discover how to observe it in their own personal and congregational way. We must ask the Holy Spirit to be our guide.

Within the First Three Days of the New Moon

The New Moon in Hebrew is called Rosh Chodesh meaning Head of the Month. The Head of the Month is the most powerful time of the Month. It is important to spend time to meet with the Lord within the first three days of the New Moon. Just as the head of a missile is the most powerful, so are the energies at the beginning of each Month. This also applies to Rosh Hashanah, the Head of the Year.

It is important to meet with the Lord at the Head, or beginning, of the Month. Seek Him during this time while the Moon is still hidden for special insight into the upcoming Month. Write down your prayer requests, goals, and Scripture for the Month.

Individual Celebration

The New Moon Celebration can be as simple as:

- Note the day the New Moon falls
- Spend quiet time with the Lord
- Seek His input and direction on the area in focus for the Month
- Ask Him to line your life up with His will in this area
- Set your direction for the Month
- Journal your prayer requests
- Speak your intentions for the upcoming Month
- Dedicate the Month to Him
- Seal it with a prayer

However, if you want to make the New Moon more of a Celebration, here are some ways to make it even more of a special time. You can adapt these suggestions for individual or group celebrations as appropriate.

Preparing for the New Moon

Mark the New Moon and Full Moon dates on your calendar.
- On the Shabbat before the next New Moon, begin to prepare your heart by reviewing and winding up the current Month
- Remember the intentions you set and note the progress you have made
- Begin to pray to the Lord and ask Him to show you the meaning of this upcoming New Moon
- Ask Him to open your understanding of His way of speaking to you about your life through the symbolisms of the Signs and Houses and how they apply to you
- Read through traditional teachings from Hebrew sources, such as *The Wisdom in the Hebrew Months,* published by Artscroll. These Bible based books will give you insight into the rich meaning each Month holds

- Based on the Zodiac Sign the New Moon is in that Month, determine the area of life that will be the focus of the New Moon.

Ceremony Suggestions

Here are some **suggestions** for observing your special time with the Lord, individually or with others in a group. Further develop your special time with the Lord as the Spirit leads. Worship can be included at the beginning, middle and end, as you are led to put this ceremony together.

~~~~~~~~~~~~~~~~~~~~~~~~

Open your time with the Sounding of the Shofar.

Sound the ram's horn at the New Moon, and when the Moon is full, on the day of our festival; this is a decree for Israel, an ordinance of the God of Jacob. Psalm 81:3-4

~~~~~~~~~~~~~~~~~~~~~~~~

Light Menorah Candles, or two separate candles. Recite the blessings over the candles. Ask His Spirit to come guide you and protect you during this special time.

~~~~~~~~~~~~~~~~~~~~~~~~

Take time to pray and seek the Lord for His insight into the traditional Biblical information surrounding the specific Month.

~~~~~~~~~~~~~~~~~~~~~~~~

What is the universal Biblical Focus of this Month based on this Months' Zodiac Sign?

How does this area apply to your life?
What personality traits are highlighted for you Month?
What lessons are there to learn?

~~~~~~~~~~~~~~~~~~~~~~~~

Look to see which House the New Moon falls in your Chart and review that area of life in more detail.

~~~~~~~~~~~~~~~~~~~~~~~~

~~~~~~~~~~~~~~~~~~~~~~~~~~~~

What area is the Lord speaking to you about and asking you to focus on in your individual Natal Chart?

~~~~~~~~~~~~~~~~~~~~~~~~~~~~

What gifts and talents can you develop this Month?
Is there something you know needs to change?
Is there an answer to a question you have about that area?

Or do you simply need to know more about how that area of life can align with the Word in order for you to have more peace and victory?

~~~~~~~~~~~~~~~~~~~~~~~~~~~~

What other areas of your life does the Holy Spirit bring to mind?

~~~~~~~~~~~~~~~~~~~~~~~~~~~~

Take a look at last Month. What have you learned?
Take a look at now. What is the current situation?
Take a look at the upcoming Month. What would you like to accomplish this Month and in future Months?

~~~~~~~~~~~~~~~~~~~~~~~~~~~~

Journal what the Lord shows you and look up Scriptures that will encourage you throughout the Month.

~~~~~~~~~~~~~~~~~~~~~~~~~~~~

Present your requests to God and set your goals and intentions for the upcoming Month. They should relate to the area of life in focus for the Month.

~~~~~~~~~~~~~~~~~~~~~~~~~~~~

Partake in Communion – Bread and Wine

~~~~~~~~~~~~~~~~~~~~~~~~~~~~

~~~~~~~~~~~~~~~~~~~~~~~~~

End with a Closing Prayer, sealing the time with the Lord

~~~~~~~~~~~~~~~~~~~~~~~~~

Fellowship meal if you are celebrating with others

~~~~~~~~~~~~~~~~~~~~~~~~~

Write notes of your conversations with the Lord and the insight He gives you during your special New Moon Celebration time. Then add any new revelation or special insights you receive throughout the Month.

Through this monthly journey, you will evaluate how you are doing in this area of life. How does your life measure up to the potential within you? As you come to new revelations you can begin to live the life you know you were meant to live. You will build confidence in yourself through God's celestial calendar. You will live your life, hand in hand with the Lord.

Special Notes for A Group Ceremony

The New MONTH Celebration
Pick a time from Molad (visible sighting of the New Moon in Jerusalem) to 14 days after (the Full Moon) to gather with friends and family to activate the goals and intentions you set in your personal New Moon Celebration. Most do this the Shabbat after the New Moon. (Note: This timing presumes you have had your personal New Moon Celebration within the first three days of the New Moon.)

Prayer and Worship
Opening prayer to sanctify the Moon
Praise, music, and thanksgiving
Psalms 33 and 148 are suggested

Blow the Shofar
Worship. A happy anticipatory tone should be set. Thank the Lord for providing us with a natural system with which to organize our lives.

Also at your times of rejoicing--your appointed festivals and New Moon feasts--you are to sound the trumpets over your burnt offerings and fellowship offerings, and they will be a memorial for you before your God. I am the LORD your God.
Numbers 10:10

Light the Candles
Light candles and recite the blessing thanking God for the lights. Thank Him for His Word, which helps us overcome the world, and the New Moon that helps guide us

Scriptural Teaching
A Scriptural teaching about the Biblical, traditional meaning, theme of the Month

Signs of the Times
If anyone knows Faith-based Astrology and can read the Signs in the Heavens, review the Faith-based interpretation of the Star Patterns for insight into the current trends that are occurring in the world. How does this current activity in the Heavens apply to our lives in general?

Set Intentions/Goals
Set goals and intentions for your group as well as for yourself based on the area of life in focus for the Month, as well as any other prayer requests you may have.

Pray for those in Authority
Pray for those in authority in your country and government.

Pray for Israel and the Peace of Jerusalem
See which area of Israel's life is in focus this Month based on their Mazal, so you can unite in prayer over it.

Bread and Wine – Communion

Dedicate the Month to the Lord

Dedicated the upcoming Month and your life, direction, and goals to the Lord. Ask Him to lead, guide, and protect throughout.

Family and Church Blessing
Ask for the LORD's special blessing on your families, children, friends, and relatives.
Ask His blessing on His Church, His Work, and to pray for the soon coming of the Messiah and God's Kingdom.

Closing Worship
Sing songs of worship and praise, again, before the evening is concluded.

Meal/Fellowship
Hold a family feast, or festive dinner after the worship as part of your celebration. We can enjoy the banquet, feast, and blessings of the table God has provided for us.

Throughout the Month
Throughout the Month, as you look up into the night sky, you will be reminded of the goals and intentions you set at New Moon Celebration.

The Lord desires for us to be intimate with Him and has this system in place so that we do stray too far from Him. Our daily prayers, morning and evening, Shabbat, the New Moon Celebrations, and the Feasts (Spring and Fall) keep us near and dear to our Lord and Savior. And through this, our lives further align with Him, and are filled with Shalom, nothing missing, nothing broken.

The Moon - Our Constant Reminder of God's Presence and Involvement in Our Lives

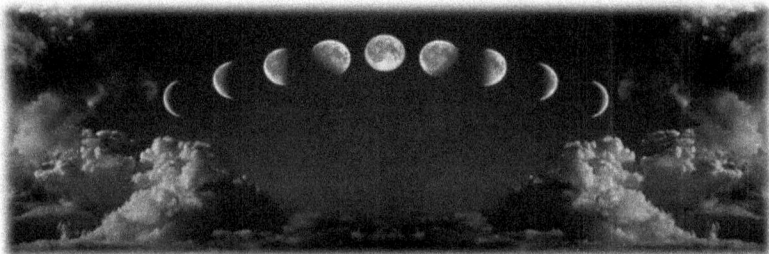

© Can Stock Photo / Korionov

The Moon above serves as a constant reminder of God's faithfulness and the creation event.

(He) who made the great lights—His love endures forever.
the sun to govern the day, His love endures forever.
the Moon and stars to govern the night:
His love endures forever.
Psalm 136:7-9

During the Month, whenever you look up and see the Moon in its different phases you can be reminded that God is always in this with you! Get a boost of His love as you remember the time you spend with Him at the New Moon Celebration, the prayer requests, and goals you set. Think of what He has shown you so far this Month! You can ponder the vastness of God and His Universe and be in awe of the fact that He knows you intimately!

This is a new celebration for Born-again, Messianic Jewish, One New Man and Third Day Believers. It is being observed as the Lord leads. It will evolve as we gain more and more understanding of the fullness of this time and as we learn to live with this new rhythm of our lives.

I invite you to be a part of this wonderful new journey! Let us purpose to join together each Month, all across the World, to celebrate our lives with the Lord, in Unity!

*"From one New Moon to another
and from one Sabbath to another, all mankind will come
and bow down before me," says the LORD.
Isaiah 66:23*

Unity of the Faith

*"...until we all reach unity in the faith and in the
knowledge of the Son of God and become mature,
attaining to the whole measure
of the fullness of Christ."
Ephesians 4:13*

"Perhaps, when we learn to follow all of God's cycles together – as One New Man in Messiah, all in one accord – we will reach the unity of the faith that God is waiting for and helping us to achieve." Revelation given by the Spirit to Rose Martin 10-24-17

Your Primary Star Pattern

Start Discovering Your Identity and Purpose!

Get your Primary Star Pattern, which will give you what you need to personally study all of the components covered in this book, *Your Destiny Discovered, Astrology for Believers*.

Learn what your Sun Sign, Moon Sign, Rising Sign are, the House your Sun is in, as well as your Chart's Ruling Planet by visiting www.YourDestinyDiscovered.com and requesting your Primary Star Pattern!

Then look through the chapters of this book again and get to know yourself in a brand-new way!

Bibliography

Research and Recommended Reading

Glean all you can from these books and leave the rest. Ask the Holy Spirit to guide you as you learn about the Heavens from God's Biblical perspective.

Bible Stories in the Stars:
Banks, William D., *The Heavens Declare: Jesus Christ Prophesied in the Stars*, Impact Christian Books, Inc., 1985, 2013
Bullinger, E. W., *The Witness of the Stars,* Kregel Publications, a division of Kregel, Inc., 1967
Fleming, Ken, *God's Voice in the Stars: Zodiac Signs and Bible Truth,* ECS Ministries, 1981
Storch, Rabbi Ari, *The Secret of the Stars,* Israel Bookshop Publications, 2011
Warner, Tim, *Mystery of the Mazzaroth: Prophecy in the Constellations,* Second Edition, 2013

Biblical Background of Astrology:
Dobin, Joel C., *To Rule Both Day and Night*, Inner Traditions International, 1977
Kronenberg, Yaakov, *Jewish Astrology, A Cosmic Science,* BN Publishing, 2015
Stephen, Susan, *Astrology for Christians,* Red Feather Mind, Body, Spirit, an imprint of Schiffer Publishing, Ltd., 2019

Natal Chart Interpretation:
Avelar, Helena and Ribeiro, Luis. *On the Heavenly Spheres: A Treatise on Traditional Astrology,* American Federation of Astrologers, Inc., 2010

Arroyo, Stephen, *Chart Interpretation Handbook: Guidelines for Understanding the Essentials of the Birth Chart,* CRCS Publications, 1989

Burk, Kevin B., *Principles of Practical Natal Astrology,* Serendipity Press, 2015

Burk, Kevin, *Astrology: Understanding the Birth Chart,* Llewellyn Publications, 2001

Crane, Joseph, *A Practical Guide to Traditional Astrology,* Archive for the Retrieval of Historical Astrological Texts, a division of Arhat Media, Inc., 1997, 2007

Dykes, Benjamin, *Traditional Astrology for Today: An Introduction,* The Cazimi Press, 2011

Frawley, John, *The Real Astrology,* Apprentice Books, 2001

George, Demetra, *Ancient Astrology: In Theory and Practice,* Rubedo Press, 2019

Greenbaum, Dorian Gieseler, *Temperament: Astrology's Forgotten Key,* The Wessex Astrologer, 2005

Hand, Robert, *Horoscope Symbols,* Whitford Press, A Division of Schiffer Publishing, 1981

Mason, Sophia, *Understanding Planetary Placements*, American Federation of Astrologers, 1993

Nicholas, Chani, *You Were Born For This: Astrology for Radical Self-Acceptance,* Harper One, An Imprint of HarperCollins Publishers, 2020

Obert, Charles, *Introduction to Traditional Natal Astrology: A Complete Working Guide for Modern Astrologers,* Almuten Press, 2015

Oken, Alan, *Complete Astrology, The Classic Guide to Modern Astrology,* Ibis Press, An Imprint of Nicolas-Has, Inc.,2006

Parker, Julia and Derek, *Parker's Astrology: The Essential Guide to Using Astrology In Your Daily Life,* DK Publishing, 1991, 2001, 2003

Sakoian, Frances and Acker, Louis S., *The Astrologer's Handbook,* Quill, An Imprint of HarperCollins Publishing, 1973

Taylor, Maxine, *Now That I've Cast It, What Do I Do With It?* 1975

Wickenburg, Joanne, *A Journey Through the Birth Chart,* American Federation of Astrologers, 1998

Woolfolk, Joanna Martine, *The Only Astrology Book You'll Ever Need,* Taylor Trade Publishing, 1982, 2006

New Moon Celebrations:

Maron, Miriam, *Ancient Moon Wisdom,* Hamilton Books, 2013

Ryzman, Zvi, *The Wisdom in the Hebrew Months: The Months, The Tribes, And the Names of Hashem,* Artscroll Series, Mesorah Publications, Ltd., 2009

Ryzman, Zvi, *The Wisdom in the Hebrew Months, Volume 2: The Months, The Constellations, The Letters, The Tribes, The Message,* Mesorah Publications, Ltd., 2014

Works Cited:

Dobin, Joel C., *To Rule Both Day and Night,* Inner Traditions International, 1977

Kronenberg, Yaakov, *Jewish Astrology, A Cosmic Science,* BN Publishing, 2015

Stephen, Susan, *Astrology for Christians,* Red Feather Mind, Body, Spirit, an imprint of Schiffer Publishing, Ltd., 2019

About the Author

Rose Martin is a Born-again Spirit-Filled Believer who has been studying and teaching the Word of God since 1986. She is an Ordained Messianic Jewish/Christian Minister, Certified Natural Health Professional (CNHP), and most recently a Faith-based Astrologer, Biblical Seer, and presenter of New Moon Celebrations.

Rose is an interpreter of the Signs in the Heavens through the Divine Science of Jewish Astrology. Her background includes, author of Eternal Life Skills, radio and on-Air tv personality, backup singer, presenter of "Exploring Life in Heaven with Rose Martin" and "Your Hebrew Roots" Torah teacher with her husband Charles. She endeavors to bring the fullness of the Lord into to all aspects of people's lives by ministering to their body, soul, and spirit. Rose is married to Charles, her husband of 36 years, is a mother of two, and grandmother of two.